REASON
TO WRITE

Douglas B. Reeves, Ph.D.

REASON TO WRITE

Help Your Child Succeed in School
and in Life Through Better
Reasoning and Clear Communication

Elementary School Edition

Kaplan Publishing
New York • London • Toronto • Sydney • Singapore

Kaplan Publishing
Published by Simon & Schuster, Inc.
1230 Avenue of the Americas
New York, NY 10020

For bulk sales to schools, colleges, and universities, please contact: Order Department, Simon & Schuster, Inc., 100 Front Street, Riverside, NJ 08075. Phone: (800) 223-2336. Fax: (800) 943-9831.

For information regarding special discounts for other bulk purchases, please contact Simon & Schuster Special Sales at 1-800-456-6798 or business@simonandschuster.com

Designed by Lisa Stokes

Manufactured in the United States of America

September 2002
10 9 8 7 6 5 4 3 2 1

Library of Congress Cataloging-in-Publication Data

ISBN: 0-7432-3045-0

Dedication

For Brooks Reeves

My favorite author, now and always

Acknowledgments

MY FIRST debt is to the parents, students, and colleagues who have shared their ideas about the importance of student writing and the methods that they have found to be most effective. It is for parents and professionals such as these that this book is written. In particular, I appreciate the thoughtful contributions of teachers in Swampscott and Marblehead, Massachusetts, who shared their insights.

Three people made contributions to this book that bridged the gap between dream and reality. Maureen McMahon of Simon & Schuster lent her wisdom and guiding hand to every page of the text. She is a human thesaurus, as well as someone who cares deeply about the written word. If there are a few instances in the following pages where the reader notices just the right word in precisely the right place, it is likely Maureen's handiwork rather than mine. Rudy Robles of Kaplan provided prodigious research skills for this project, including an exhaustive review of state writing standards, state scoring guides, and research on student writing. Allison Schumacher provided extensive contributions to the chapters on creative and analytical writing and reviewed every word of the text.

Student contributors, both named and anonymous, provided realistic examples for several chapters. James, Sophie, Michael, Rachel, and their friends are courageous and smart kids. They shared not only their best work, but their work in progress. At a tender age they have reminded me of the value of trial and error and the necessity of a second effort.

Lucy McCormick Calkins of Columbia University is the best teacher of writing I know. A generation of schoolchildren is fortunate to have teachers influenced by Professor Calkins's passion, intelligence, and vulnerability. More than a million children call themselves writers because Lucy convinced their teachers that the literary life is as noble a calling for an elementary schoolchild as it was for Hemingway. Every time I reread her memoir, *Lessons from a Child,* my eyes well with tears of recognition and gratitude.

My family regularly reminds me that high tide is more exciting than my eleventh book, that bedtime reading is more important than a media interview, that a paper buried in the backpack is more important than a fact buried in the newspaper, that every performance of every play deserves an audience, and that every school board candidate needs someone to stuff envelopes. Brooks, Alex, Julia, and James are my anchors. Shelley is my safe harbor, whose wit and love make every trip home the best part of the journey. Julie Reeves enters her eightieth year generously sharing her passion for learning with her grandchildren. J. B. Reeves bequeathed a legacy of the joy of inquiry, the inheritors of which were not only his progeny but his students. These people are my family, and they are my reasons to write.

dr
Swampscott, Massachusetts

Contents

1 Why Is Writing So Important?

THE SCHOOLS our children attend today are different from those of a generation ago. The difference between our memories of elementary school and today's reality for our children can lead to conflicting emotions. On the one hand, we want our children to have more opportunities, better education, and a more sound preparation for the rigors of secondary school than we had. On the other hand, many parents occasionally wish that today's schools were more familiar, with a little less structure, fewer tests, and more fun.

Never before have there been such high expectations for all children—not just a few—for greater performance in more academic areas. Many parents of children in elementary school today recall their own early experiences with writing as a series of creative stories and neatly stapled book reports, each returned with a smiley face and a letter grade, and perhaps an encouraging remark about our neat handwriting or our effort. In the general scheme of things, the importance of writing fell somewhere after reading and math, and the "rules" certainly seemed a lot fuzzier. Certain things were clear—we had to begin our sentences with capital letters, and every sentence needed to end with a period or a question mark or an exclamation point—but many things were not. What were the hallmarks of a "good" story? Why did the book report we worked so hard on only earn a B? Somehow we muddled through without ever really understanding the rules.

The expectations for our children are very different. Creative stories are sandwiched between requirements for persuasive and analytical essays.

Requirements for spelling, grammar, and punctuation are accompanied by demands for transitions, word choice, research, technology applications, and a consideration of the writer's audience. Because the expectations for performance are new, parents such as Barbara Simpson find a wide gulf between what she regards as acceptable school performance and what teachers, school districts, and state education officials have determined are the requirements for her daughter's success.

Barbara enjoys the daily routine she calls "mining the backpack." After supper, she unzips Kristin's backpack and removes the day's papers, cookie crumbs, and messages to parents. Recently, along with the calendars and lunch menus, she found a form with the words KRISTIN ANNE SIMPSON—STATE WRITING TEST REPORT emblazoned across the top in formal block type. Her eyes scanned the results. "What do they mean she is *progressing?*" Barbara asked herself. A fourth grader, Kristin, had always received A's and B's, and she particularly enjoyed writing. Now Barbara suspected that something was wrong. While the meaning of "progressing" was not clear from the report, she knew that it was not at all the same as "advanced" or "proficient." Barbara had never considered the possibility that Kristin was doing any less than what was expected of a fourth grader. Her desk was neat, her homework completed on time, and her parent-teacher conferences always full of good news. The messages were inconsistent, and Barbara knew that there were more state writing tests in the years ahead.

This was not Barbara's first encounter with the new school requirements for writing. Last year, when Kristin's brother, Michael, was in the fifth grade, he brought home a science report that had corrections in spelling and punctuation. His social studies reports were graded not only for content, but also for written expression. "Why are they grading English in a science project?" she wondered. She recalled viewing with pride Michael's elaborate maps of Africa and his history timelines for his social studies classes, and then sharing his disappointment when his writing skills were part of his evaluation. Now in his first year of middle school, Michael is facing the same demands. "Writing across the curriculum," his teachers call it. Whatever the label, Barbara thought, school is a lot different today than it was twenty years ago.

As a child, Barbara enjoyed writing. She remembers receiving her first diary for her ninth birthday and how much she loved keeping her thoughts in it. She still did that and was delighted that Kristin was doing the same thing. An official announcement that the quality of Kristin's writing was somehow deficient might extinguish the creative spark that Barbara wanted to nourish. Kristin's teacher applauded her writing, invariably attaching stars, rainbows, and kind comments to every story. "I've got to get to the bottom of this," Barbara said to herself. Then the nightly mining of the backpack revealed another paper, this one with the principal's photocopied signature at the bottom.

"Please join me for an informal discussion of student achievement in our school," the invitation from the principal began. "I always enjoy hearing from parents about their views of student performance. I will also be happy to answer your questions about standards and testing, including any concerns you may have about the new state writing test. Refreshments will be served."

He wants to hear my views? Barbara thought. He didn't ask my opinion last year when all these new things started. I can't believe all the stuff they want kids to do today. It's not enough that Kristin reads better than other fourth graders and does fine in math. The report from school said that she needs to write essays—in fourth grade! Frankly, I'm not sure if they need all that. I never had to write essays until high school. If the principal really wants to hear from parents, I'll be there. This stuff is getting out of hand. There's nothing wrong with my daughter, she concluded. Why are they making her take these writing tests anyway? Why can't writing just be fun?

Barbara deserves an answer, and her principal must come up with something more persuasive than "The state department of education requires it." Parents across the nation are noticing that student writing requirements are changing in content, frequency, and importance. Although the reasons to write may be clear to educational researchers, the rationale is not clear for many parents. Let us consider four fundamental reasons why every student should write frequently:

1. Writing improves reading comprehension.
2. Writing improves student performance in other academic areas, including social studies, science, and mathematics.
3. Writing contributes to a sense of connection and personal efficacy by participation in society.
4. Writing, particularly with evaluation, editing, revision, and rewriting, will improve the ability of a student to communicate and succeed on state and local writing tests.

WRITING IMPROVES READING

The connection between writing and reading is subtle. Some parents and more than a few teachers assume that literacy development is a linear sequence, beginning with speaking, proceeding to reading, and ending with writing. "Do you really expect students to begin writing before they are proficient readers?" comes the inevitable challenge. In a word, yes. In fact, students will not become proficient readers unless they begin writing about what they have read.

Ask your child these questions: "What makes for a good reader?" "How are good readers different from kids who are not such good readers?" You are likely to hear responses such as the following:

> *"A good reader knows all the words."*
> *"A good reader says the words correctly."*
> *"A good reader can read very fast."*
> *"A good reader reads big books."*

If the same question is put to teachers, however, you are likely to hear a quite different definition. The importance of comprehension, including the ability to summarize text and draw inferences from facts presented in the text, will dominate the discussion. While this may seem obvious in the abstract, it is not obvious to the parent who has just been told that her child needs extra help in reading. "What do you mean that she's not a good reader? She reads to me every night flawlessly!" The statement is true. Unfortunately, the child reads flawlessly because the story, repeated night after night, has been memorized. The parent listens approvingly, but enunciation of words and comprehension of ideas remain two distinct abilities.

Writing can help bridge the gap between decoding words and understanding their meaning. Your child's ability to write a summary or a reflective response to what he has read will provide you with valuable feedback about how well he understands what he is reading. The process of writing will help your child explore his ideas about what he has read. The reading-writing connection will be discussed at greater length in chapter 4.

WRITING IMPROVES PERFORMANCE IN ALL ACADEMIC AREAS

The second argument for more student writing is the improvement of academic performance in every other academic area. Student performance is typically measured in the classroom, through the assignment of grades and through the administration of state or district tests. On both of these indicators of student performance, more frequent student writing is associated with improved performance. Interestingly, students who write more frequently perform better not only on essay exams or other tests that require student writing, but also on multiple-choice tests across a range of subjects. This is great news for parents who have been concerned about excessive test preparation in schools or the replacement of thinking and reasoning in the curriculum with activities that they equate with test gamesmanship. When students engage in frequent writing, particularly with specific feedback, editing, and revision, they are building their reasoning and thinking skills. While parents on both sides of the emotional school testing issue may disagree about the value and appropriateness of testing, they should find common ground on the elevation of thinking and reasoning skills over test prep. If you detest the idea of school becoming an academic boot camp filled with six hours a day of practice multiple-choice test questions, then you should support student writing for its engagement, interest, and fun. If you worry about your child's performance in the world of high-stakes testing, then you too should support student writing, because it is the skill most directly related to improved scores in reading, social studies, science, and even mathematics.

The reason for the strong relationship between writing and test performance is unclear, but it probably relates to the relationship between writing and thinking. In order to write well, students must think in a logical manner, proceeding from beginning, to middle, to end. They must think in an analytical manner, considering similarities and differences. Thus, when they write well, they think well. And when students think well, they perform better in any context.

WRITING IS ESSENTIAL FOR COMMUNICATION IN A DEMOCRACY

The third response to the question, Why write? lies at the heart of our relationship with other individuals and institutions in our society. Citizens have influence only to the extent that they use it, and writing transforms an important but silent idea into a powerful source of influence. Legislators and policy makers are routinely deluged with mail. They can tell the difference between the form letters and the rare notes that are crafted by a constituent who cared enough about an issue to write persuasively and passionately. State legislators and United States senators, mayors and presidents, governors and cabinet secretaries can all tell the difference between these two methods of expression. Students and other citizens must write to a specific audience and must write with a purpose. One of the most important activities described in this book is the composition of letters for public officials. When students are passionate, they are more likely to write with feeling, clarity, and persuasive impact. Whether you have a first grader who is worried about the preservation of a local park, a third grader concerned about the purity of the water, or a fifth grader who has strong opinions about terrorism and war, now is the time to lay the foundation for the use of compelling prose as a right and responsibility of citizens in a free society. The first time that your child receives a letter from a member of Congress or other public official, you will witness the birth of a committed author of letters to public officials. The response will not contain a sea of red ink or critical remarks about the rules of grammar. Responses from public officials are usually respectful and indicate that the letter authored by your child was taken seriously. Of the many keys to student motivation, one of the most important is efficacy, the perception by students that their personal efforts have an impact and can influence the actions of others. Writing letters that elicit a response is a practice that nurtures efficacy and, as a result, fosters motivation in the student writer. Chapter 10 considers the writing of letters, and chapter 13 provides some practical ideas for the creation of persuasive essays.

There is a power in persuasive writing that extends beyond influencing public policy. Every time students write, they rekindle the spark that says, "My words matter." A generation ago, I recall my wide-eyed response at the letter from the governor of Massachusetts in response to my request for information as part of a second-grade project. As I write this chapter, my eight-year old son is close by, carefully crafting the letter he will send to the president of the United States. It is part of a Cub Scout project in which the children have raised money to help Afghan children. Each student will send not only money, but also ideas, appreciation, and good wishes.

Writing also builds a bridge from those who receive the protections that our society offers to those who provide those protections. Before children take the initiative to write, the two parties are linked by an abstract social bargain. After an exchange of letters, there are names, families, faces, and feelings that link the public servants of a democracy and its beneficiaries. There are many soldiers who celebrate holidays alone and whose loneliness is temporarily relieved by letters from schoolchildren. Firefighters, police officers, and other public safety professionals have received letters with which they decorate their walls, displaying the written expressions of love, hope, and appreciation from children.

The opportunities for students to express themselves in a democracy include not only correspondence with government officials, but with other institutions whose decisions affect the daily lives of children. Think of the ways your child interacts with a local business owner, physician, or librarian, each of whom could be influenced in their decisions by a student's carefully written letter. Consider the last time your child was dissatisfied with a purchase and a victim of deceptive advertising. A letter might be the perfect way for your child to state her grievance and request a remedy. If, on the other hand, your child has been particularly delighted with the courtesy of a store owner, the kindness of a doctor, or the brilliance of a toy design, a letter expressing these sentiments will also make an impression.

WRITING IMPROVES WRITING

This may sound obvious, but the process of writing, editing, and rewriting will help your child become a better writer. If I were writing a book about basketball, the following comment would not seem particularly insightful: "The way to improve shooting free throws is to shoot more free throws." The insight is less obvious when the subject is the act of taking pen in hand to commit ideas to paper. Writing is so easily avoided, and the demands for writing are so infrequent that very bright children can emerge from elementary school with good reading skills, splendid social skills, and superb academic gamesmanship, and yet face the prospect of entering their middle-school years as dreadful writers. That gap between the demands of secondary school and the meager writing skills possessed by these students will undermine their self-confidence and motivation, with detrimental impact on every subject.

Students will not become better writers through tricks or sleight of hand. They will become better writers by writing more frequently and, most important, critically reviewing their work, revising it, and getting detailed feedback from other writers, including fellow students, teachers, and parents. Watch children engaged in an activity that they find satisfying and at which they succeed. Whether it is basketball, music, field hockey, or art, these activities share common characteristics. Students know the rules of the game, and the definition of success is clear. Students help one another with encouragement and correction. Teachers and coaches also know the criteria for success, and thus give students consistent messages about their performance. Success is achieved incrementally. The novice does not instantly acquire the skills of Michael Jordan or Arthur Rubinstein, but rather shoots just one more basket or plays one more correct note. So it is with writing. The trick for parents is to find ways to create the same level of excitement and engagement in writing that children find in other rewarding activities.

WHEN YOUR CHILD IS FRUSTRATED WITH WRITING

As you work through the ideas in this book, you can anticipate your child's occasional frustrations. The words won't come out quite right the first time. The ideas will be wonderful, but the penmanship illegible. The paragraph might be perfect, but the computer may crash. What was an exciting project a few minutes before will suddenly become the source of criticism, confrontation, and tears. When these inevitable frustrations arise, step back and consider why we are devoting time to writing. Whether your child is writing a movie review, a science report, a letter to a grandparent, an argument to be delivered to a public official, or any of the many writing projects in the chapters to follow, the power, joy, improved reading, and excellent writing that will result from these activities must be weighed against the occasional frustrations. To keep the power of positive writing experiences clearly in evidence, consider a "wall of fame" for your child's best writing projects. A bulletin board or a special folder can serve this purpose. Whatever format you use, the response to inevitable frustrations need not be confrontation and tests of wills, but rather a recollection of success and the extraordinary emotional satisfaction associated with your child's best writing experiences.

Why Do Some Students Dislike Writing?

EVERY PARENT has witnessed this scene: A bright and creative child who was enthusiastically engaged in a homework assignment only moments ago has suddenly transformed into a sullen, angry, and rebellious brat.

"I hate this!" the child rages. "I just don't get it. Why do you make me feel so stupid? I quit!"

What happened? we wonder, as joy turns to anxiety and giggles become tears. In an unsettlingly clinical manner, we are witnessing the perfect experiment in child psychology. In this situation, many of the factors frequently associated with childhood behavior—parenting, diet, home environment, climate, and sibling relationships—have all been relatively stable, at least within the past ten minutes or so. However, one thing has changed: The homework assignment was out of the ordinary. The joy-filled expert became the misery-laden novice. Anxiety replaced confidence.

The culprit is not the homework assignment itself, but the conditions surrounding it. Consider a practical example that almost every parent has witnessed early in the life of a baby: walking. What accompanies the first tentative baby step? Encouragement, enticement, and enthusiasm at the slightest hint of a hesitant step. Parents applaud, siblings brag, grandparents take pictures and post them on the refrigerator door. What happens when the baby falls down? I am not aware of a single instance in which the grandparents, in sullen disgrace, removed the baby's pictures from the refrigerator or the parents concluded, "That child just isn't a walker." On the contrary, each "failure" is met with encouragement, commitment, and ever more enthusiasm for each successive attempt at walking. Similarly, every parent who has applauded a toddler's successful venture into the bathroom understands the point. In a child's early years, we are effusive and specific in our praise. As they grow older, children miss such affirmation; so do parents.

Between the transition from crawler to walker and the first day of elementary school, there are lessons learned and lessons forgotten. The lessons learned by the child include the following:

- Success is applauded, and it feels great.
- Failure is a temporary and inevitable step toward future success—at least for really important endeavors such as walking and using the potty.
- I would rather keep trying than disappoint my parents.

The lessons forgotten by the parents include the following:

- Praise is more effective than criticism.
- Specific and meaningful praise ("She made three whole steps today!") is more effective than unspecific praise of questionable meaning ("Why, he looks just like his father!" or "You're great!").
- First attempts at new activities are rarely spontaneous, but the result of encouragement, direction, and modeling.

We know that some students do not like writing, particularly the academic writing required in school. Before we conclude that the cause for this distaste is the fault of the student or teacher, let us consider some alternate factors. Think of the last time you looked at a piece of writing your child brought home from school. What was the first thing that you noticed? On the spot, you may say, "I immediately noticed the improvements my child made compared to her previous assignment, praised her for those specific improvements, and warmly encouraged another attempt at a similar writing assignment." As the kids say, "Yeah, right." My great joy is to live with four young critics who are, above all, authentic in their dialogue with parents. They might respond to the theoretical parent response in the following terms:

"Wait a minute! You didn't notice what I did right. In fact, the first thing you noticed was the marks made by the teacher. You focused on my mistakes, not my successes. In fact, I made some mistakes that were overlooked by the teacher, and you pointed those out as well. By the time you and the teacher were finished with my written work, there was no doubt that my writing was unsatisfactory. What makes you think that I want to make yet another futile attempt?"

Okay. I confess. I have never heard any of my children express the preceding sentiments. But I have heard them say, "I can't do this!" within seconds of my well-intentioned review of their work. This response is provoked whenever I fail to recall the lessons of a few years ago. When my enthusiasm over the first step, the first word, and yes, the first successful venture to the potty is replaced by the professor's critical eye, my children respond with frustration and self-doubt.

In the penultimate scene of the Broadway hit *The Music Man*—the scene before the triumphant marching band blares "76 Trombones Led the Big Parade"—the parents hear a tuneless assembly of novice band members wail through a rendition of Bach's Minuet in G.

"That's my boy!" exclaims one parent.

"It's beautiful!" calls out another.

Professor Hill has delivered on his promise after all, and parents hear beauty in one sour note after another. So also I can suspend almost fifty years of training as a classical musician and hear my eight-year-old play the cello and, at my best, respond to each note as I would to his first steps. I applaud. I smile. I revel in every note that approximates the correct tone. At my worst, I interrupt with looks of disapproval and notice failures more than successes. I forget that the journey to the triumphant "76 Trombones" was preceded by the atonal Minuet in G.

Let us now confront the inevitable challenge from those who contend that the emphasis on praise over criticism is a misguided attempt to spare the student's feelings. Let's look again at our novice walker. We do not lecture a child about the error of the fall after the first step, nor do we respond to the fall by saying, "In the twenty-first century, sitting is a perfectly acceptable way to get around, and I certainly would not want to impose my will on this child." Instead, we encouraged, coached, cajoled, praised, and encouraged some more. We help our children achieve success with neither criticism nor a suspension of our expectations, but with a recognition of the obvious—"You wanted to walk, but you are now sitting down"—and encouragement, including our open arms at the conclusion of a journey of a few seconds. In brief, we have clear expectations, and we offer immediate feedback and loads of positive reinforcement.

Many of us succumb to the temptation to lecture a child about the error of a flawed writing assignment. After a few seconds of effort, we replace encouragement with the command "Finish your homework" and the expectation that we will see a flawless result. We supplant the promise of immediate feedback with the uncertainty of inconsistent, subjective evaluation. Yesterday it was the spelling, but today it is the grammar. Wherever the child places the emphasis, there is something missing. Few of us make the same error in response to our child's musical efforts. When our young violinist is not Paganini, we applaud. When our young pianist is not Van Cliburn, we cheer. When our young writer is not Hemingway, we lecture. We need not be oblivious of errors in student writing, but we can nevertheless applaud. We can applaud rich description in the absence of proper spelling. We can applaud meaningful transitions in the absence of superlative grammar. We can applaud coherent organization in the absence of flawless punctuation. Above all, we want our young writer to come back to the task, to persevere, to achieve the emotional skill of resilience. As parents, we do not want our children to become complacent or defeated. We desire children who are resilient, who in every task before them perceive at least 51 percent competence and less than 49 percent failure. When we fail to achieve or exceed that equation, we have an unmotivated child. More to the point, we have failed to remember the lessons our children taught us when they took their first steps.

What Should My Child Know and Be Able to Do?

Before your child graduates from elementary school, she must be able to:

write a research paper, including a bibliography;
write a persuasive essay, supported by evidence;
write an analytical essay in literature, science, social studies, and the arts;
write a descriptive essay, using details imagery;
write creatively, including short stories and poems;
write legibly by hand and use a word processor;
write using the conventions of English grammar, punctuation, and spelling.

Students today must write more frequently, in more different subjects, with greater sophistication, using more research, and with more accuracy than ever before. Because the research evidence suggests that writing is an important and helpful skill for children of all ages, these requirements are a great thing. Students who leave elementary school able to meet the writing requirements listed above will enter secondary school with confidence and success. There is, however, one significant problem. In many schools there is not a clear progression of skill development from kindergarten through the fifth and sixth grades. As a result, the most difficult requirements tend to land in the last year or two of elementary school. For students who are well prepared, those years are challenging but reasonable. For students whose early elementary school years did not include extensive writing, fifth and sixth grades can be a disaster.

Straight-A students whose backpacks were routinely filled with smiley faces in second and third grade find fifth grade full of strange and unfamiliar requirements.

To replace frustration and anger in the later grades with the self-confidence of a successful student, children must have parents and teachers who build their skills over time. If your school does not make these requirements a priority, then it is essential that you help your child build these skills at home. The attitude that "they'll get that later on"—perhaps in eighth grade or high school—is a prescription for a frustrated and unsuccessful student. Even if your child's school does not have these requirements now, it will soon. The time to prepare your child is now.

Many of the official literacy curriculum documents can seem overwhelming. In order to address every state standard and cover every conceivable need for students, these documents become unwieldy and unrealistic. One study by Dr. Robert Marzano and his colleagues at Mid-continent Research for Education and Learning suggested that schools in many states would need to more than double the number of school days available if they were to fully address every state standard. Therefore, this chapter does not contain a laundry list of every possible requirement. Rather, the following pages provide a set of "safety net standards"—essential knowledge for your child in the elementary grades. One of the national leaders in the creation of safety net standards is Dr. Terry Thompson and his colleagues in the Wayne Township Metropolitan School District in Indiana. After a comprehensive review of national and state standards, as well as the best available language arts curriculum documents, they created a short list of essential skills for every grade. This effort, led by Deputy Superintendent Dr. Karen Gould and language arts coordinator Carole Erlandson, with contributions by teachers and administrators throughout the district, forms the basis of this chapter. It is important to note that this is not an exhaustive writing curriculum for any student. Rather, this represents the essentials every student should master. It is very likely that your child's school will require more than the following requirements. However, if your child's school requires less, it is imperative that parental coaching close the gap between the school curriculum and these essentials.

Kindergarten

Your kindergartener should be able to

recognize and name all capital and lowercase letters of the alphabet;

write using pictures, letters, and words;

draw pictures and write words for a specific reason;

write capital and lowercase letters of the alphabet, correctly shaping and spacing the letters.

Grade 1

Your first grader should be able to

write brief narratives (stories) describing an experience;

write in complete sentences;

retell stories using basic story grammar and relating the sequence of story events by answering who, what, when, where, why, and how questions;

print legibly.

Grade 2

Your second grader should be able to

organize related ideas together to maintain a consistent focus;

use a simple graphic organizer, such as a story web or time line, to demonstrate an understanding of the elements of a story;

write a brief description of a familiar object, person, place, or event;

write a paragraph that develops a main idea and use details to support the main idea;

distinguish between complete and incomplete sentences;

print legibly.

Grade 3

Your third grader should be able to

determine the theme of an author's message in fiction and nonfiction text;

demonstrate an understanding of the theme or message by writing an accurate summary of the text;

use pre-writing strategies, including web, list, and outline;

create a first draft, edit and revise the draft, and create a second draft;

edit the work of other students, suggesting improvements and identifying errors;

create single paragraphs with topic sentences and simple supporting facts and details;

write descriptive pieces about people, places, things, or experiences;

develop a unified main idea and use details to support the main idea;

write complete sentences of statement, command, question, or exclamation, using appropriate final punctuation;

write legibly in printing or in cursive.

Grade 4

Your fourth grader should be able to

write informational pieces with three or more paragraphs, including an introductory paragraph, supporting paragraphs with details, and a conclusion that summarizes the essay;

write paragraphs with a central idea contained in a topic sentence at or near the beginning of the paragraph;

use correct indentation of paragraphs, as well as proper spelling, grammar, and punctuation;

demonstrate a recognition of audience, including the use of letters, essays designed to persuade, and essays designed to give directions;

create interesting sentences by using words that describe, explain, or provide additional details;

identify and use adjectives and adverbs;

summarize written text of approximately four hundred words by providing a legible written summary that is accurate and in order;

analyze two different written texts, correctly identifying similarities and differences;

write legibly in printing and in cursive;

use a word processor to create a paragraph, save, print, and edit a document.

Grade 5

Your fifth grader should be able to

write informational pieces with five or more paragraphs;

present important ideas or events in sequence or in chronological order;

provide details in supporting paragraphs and include transitions linking paragraphs;

write a research report about important ideas, issues, or events. The research paper includes a narrowly framed question that directs the research and an outline of the paper; uses a variety of information sources, including firsthand interviews, reference materials, and electronic resources; a first and second draft, and a bibliography; demonstrate an understanding of the requirements of academic integrity by complete and accurate citations of sources;

identify and correctly use appropriate tense (present, past, past participle);

write legibly in cursive and print;

use a word processor to create a paragraph, save, print, and edit a document;

create and include in a paper a chart, table, or graph in two forms: a word processed document and a hand-drawn document.

Appendix A includes the grade-by-grade writing standards used in the state of California. The California Content Standards provides one of the most complete and easily understood sets of grade-level expectations in the nation. Appendix A also includes Web site addresses for each state's English language arts standards, which include requirements for writing. When reviewing your state's requirements for writing, it is important to remember that all standards do not have equal weight. If your state has an elementary writing test, the guide (or rubric) used to score the test (also available on the state Web site) will provide you with important clues about which standards carry the most weight. It's also a good idea to ask your child's teacher how the state's writing requirements are addressed in his or her classroom, and from grade to grade throughout the school.

4 The Reading-Writing Connection

"**YOU ARE SUCH** a good reader!" exclaimed Stephen's grandma. "You said every word correctly. And you read so quickly! You must be the best reader in the second grade!"

This affirmation was music to Stephen's ears. He agreed that he was a good reader, despite some recent trouble in school. Grandma's enthusiasm settled the matter, at least in the boy's judgment. Stephen's mother, Katy, however, was puzzled. Until recently, she had shared Grandma's assumptions about Stephen's nightly race through *Hop on Pop* and *The Cat in the Hat,* books she remembered reading as a young child to the enthusiastic approval of her own mother, Stephen's grandma. Along with these pleasant memories came the recollection that the approval she received at home was inconsistent with reading problems her teachers described on her report cards.

Decades later, Katy once again attempted to reconcile her impression of reading competence with unsettling reports of reading difficulty. Katy looked at a recent report on Stephen's reading scores with terms such as "comprehension," "inferences," "summarization," and "vocabulary." The report said that Stephen's reading scores were well below the second-grade level. How do they know that? she wondered. Any kid can have a bad day. It must be one of those standardized test problems. But Stephen's mom also noticed some other trouble signs, including incomplete assignments and Stephen's discomfort whenever she asked him to talk about the stories he'd read. The note on the report card that "Stephen needs to focus much more on his reading" was the last straw. We *are* focusing on reading, she thought. We read every night! What more are we supposed to be doing?

WHAT DOES "GOOD READING" REALLY MEAN?

Katy's exasperation is completely understandable. Not only does she want to believe that her child is a good reader, but she honestly believes that she has been an active supporter of the development of his reading skills. Her own experiences in second grade are now flooding back. She recalls the sustained applause for every memorized poem she recited and each book that she read after dinner. She loved these performances during which she would read loudly and quickly, and she particularly loved the enthusiastic praise. Katy would turn the pages dramatically, with everyone knowing that she was doing so only for show, the words on the page having long since been memorized. Applause after dinner, however, was contradicted by concern at school. Katy's "reading problem" was, her mother firmly declared, just a misunderstanding. Now that Stephen faced the same situation, Katy needed to get to the bottom of the matter.

Just what is good reading, anyway? she wondered. How will I know if Stephen is a good reader? How can I help him?

THE READING PYRAMID: LETTERS, WORDS, IDEAS, AND EXPLORATION

Although academic researchers frequently insist that reading is an exceptionally complex cognitive process that requires an appropriately complex vocabulary and analytical structure, most parents are not interested in the deeper implications of "phonemic awareness" and "metacognition." We just want to know if our kids can read well. The Reading Pyramid (Figure 4.1) is a simple way for parents and children to think about reading, progressing from the simple to the complex. The short answer to Katy's question What is good reading? is this: Good readers have climbed the pyramid. They know their letters and words, as Katy surely did in her primary years and as Stephen does today. They also understand the ideas that the words convey and can explore those ideas, drawing conclusions from the facts before them and making predictions based on the information in the text.

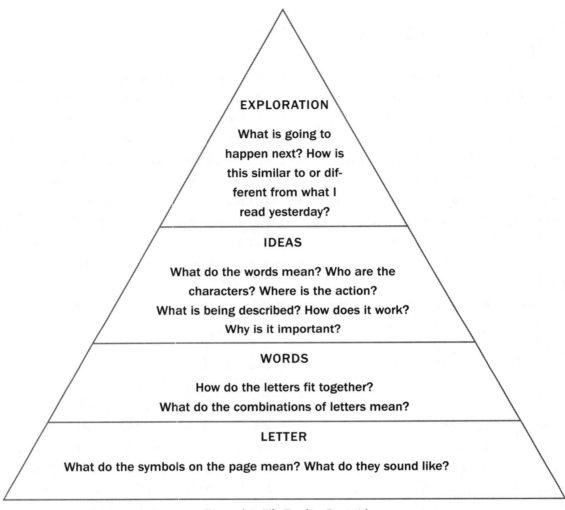

Figure 4.1 The Reading Pyramid

As the base, or the bottom, of the Reading Pyramid indicates, Stephen has accomplished what is vital to become a successful reader: He can read words. There is nothing wrong with reading aloud, memorizing poems and stories, and receiving enthusiastic applause from loving parents, grandparents, and anyone else willing to listen. Stephen has successfully climbed part of the Reading Pyramid. Had he and his parents heeded the counsel of the so-called experts and attempted to gather the meaning of words by intuition, he might as well have confronted an Egyptian pyramid and stared endlessly at hieroglyphics.

Grandma's enthusiasm built the bottom of the pyramid, and she deserves our appreciation. In order to promote Stephen's development as a successful reader, Katy's next step should be to help him make the transition from words to ideas, and from ideas to exploration. To achieve that transition, Stephen must write. Specifically, he must write about what he has read in such a way that he develops an understanding of the ideas expressed in the text and is able to explore those ideas, making comparisons and predictions. In brief, Stephen must move from saying the words to understanding them, from reading quickly to reading deeply.

WHAT KIND OF WRITING IS IMPORTANT?

There are several types of writing that students must master. These types of writing, sometimes labeled genres, each serve different purposes. The most frequently assigned type of writing in elementary school is the narrative. The essence of narrative is telling a story, and it is a wonderful way for students to let their creativity soar. Characters emerge from their inventive minds and, for a brief moment, the kids are in charge. The adult characters do what they are told and, in their child-created dialogue, express themselves precisely as the writer hears them.

As important as the narrative is, it is insufficient as the primary basis for student writing, particularly when we are attempting to make the reading-writing connection. The type of writing most closely related to the improvement of student reading skills is the creation of a clear and accurate summary of a story, article, chapter, or book that the student has read. This does not imply that stories and personal narratives should be stopped, but that schools should increase the number of written summaries that students perform. For example, some schools devote a daily time to reading, frequently called DEAR—Drop Everything And Read. Other schools label this time allocated to personal reading as Sustained Silent Reading. Some teachers greatly enhance the value of this classroom time by replacing the twenty minutes of unstructured reading with fifteen minutes of self-selected reading followed by a five-minute written summary. This practice preserves the student's power of individual choice, but adds the power of written summaries to improve the student's reading comprehension.

There are three key intellectual skills that students develop when they write about what they have read: summarization, analysis, and prediction. Together, these skills form the basis for reading comprehension. With them, students can master difficult text in any field. Without them, students are decoding syllables without understanding.

Summarization

Summarization is a journalistic account in response to the questions that begin with the words *who, what, when, where,* and *why.* This is a particularly important skill for increasing comprehension when the text is complex, unfamiliar, or boring. The command to "Read chapter four" in a social studies textbook does not accomplish very much unless the students comprehend what they have read. Homework assignments that involve reading without a check for understanding have the potential to waste a great deal of time and create frustration for students, teachers, and parents. "I did my homework!" the student proclaims.

"That's not what it looks like according to your report card," the parent responds.

"But I did do it, really. You just don't believe me," cries the child, and the tears begin to flow.

This unfortunate confrontation is caused by the gulf between what a child thinks "good reading" means and her ability to comprehend and summarize information on the printed page. To close this gap, parents should replace the question, "Did you do your homework?" with this requirement: "I'm so pleased that you read that chapter. Let's take a minute to show me what you know. First, write down the most important things that you remember about the chapter."

Thus begins a habit that will sustain a child in elementary school, through college, postgraduate education, and the world beyond. This is the habit of summarizing difficult text in one's own words. There are legions of college students who identify their academic turning point from mediocrity and bewilderment to success and confidence as the day that they started writing summaries of chapters or parts of chapters in books. They had always taken notes on lectures, summarizing and organizing what they had heard. But when they applied this same level of organization and intellectual understanding to the printed word, their success, confidence, and understanding soared. At this point, we are not asking for advanced analysis, but only for the lowest level of comprehension in the form of a summarization of what the text says. The first time that parents request such a summary, they should expect some challenge from the child such as, "But I already read this!" Their gentle encouragement must be consistent but firm, "I know that you read it, and that's wonderful. But I want to hear about this in your words, so let's write it out and talk about it." I have seen children, including my own, return to the text for a thorough reading. The hasty enunciation of words is now replaced by a thoughtful examination of the text. When the expectation for comprehension and understanding is clear, students will stop, ask questions, get definitions, and persist for full understanding. Within minutes, they know that letters and words are not enough. To understand the ideas before them, they must think as they read, question as their eyes pass over the words, and organize the material so that the ideas become not merely a presentation by the author, but a collaboration between reader and writer.

The Guide for Summarization (Figure 4.2) provides an outline for this process. This form may be reproduced and used as a guide for summarizing any type of reading, from homework assignments to the stories you read together for fun. A sample completed form is provided (Figure 4.3) to illustrate its use.

GUIDE FOR SUMMARIZATION

Who? (List the people involved in this story, chapter, or article.)

_____

_____

What? (What were they doing?)

_____

_____

Where? (Describe the setting. Tell us the location and describe it in your own words.)

_____

_____

When? (When did the action happen – past, present, or future? What else do you know about this time?)

_____

_____

Why? (Why were the characters acting as they did?)

_____

_____

Figure 4.2 Guide For Summarization

SUMMARY: DANNY'S GREAT ESCAPE

Who? Danny Boyleston and his dad.

What? Danny and his father had just come in from playing baseball. They were very tired so they went upstairs to get ready for bed. They were watching television in the third floor of their house when they smelled smoke. A fire had started in the first floor. Even though the fire truck came, the whole house burned down. Danny lost everything he had, even his books and games. They just ran down the stairs and couldn't go back up again to save anything.

Where? The house is very old. Danny says it is over 100 years old and is a historic place. The house is very close to other old buildings, but none of the other buildings were burned. The house is on a busy street, but nobody seemed to see the smoke at first.

When? They think the fire started about 8:30 or so at night, but Danny and his Dad didn't smell it until after 9 o'clock. Danny was already in his PJ's.

Why? Even though the fire truck came quickly, there was nothing that could be done. You would think that Danny and his Dad would be very sad, but they were not so sad. At first, the fire investigators thought Danny might have set the fire playing with matches. They noticed that fire started inside the house and that no one on the street noticed the fire. Then Danny noticed the burned wires by the lamp hanging from the ceiling. The fire inspector knew that it was the electrical wiring that caused the fire and not Danny. Danny was relieved and said he would just have to get some different clothes and toys. Most of all, he was happy that his Dad was safe and so was he.

Figure 4.3 Complete Guide For Summarization

Beyond Summarization: Analysis

Once students have a firm grasp of the facts in the text, they have satisfied the journalist's desire to know who, what, when, where, and why. The next level of reading comprehension involves analysis. The essence of analysis is the classic beginning of the essay question, "Compare and contrast . . ." What do those requirements really mean? Although every secondary school student must master the requirements for the "compare and contrast" question, we rarely prepare elementary students for the enormous leap from summarization to analysis. Nevertheless, if we use appropriate vocabulary and ask the right questions, elementary school students can develop the intellectual skills involved in analysis. The question should be asked in a way that students are more likely to understand. For example, "How is this story [or chapter or poem] similar to the one we read yesterday? How is it different?" The Analysis Form (Figure 4.4) provides a useful way for students to analyze work, systematically listing similarities and differences. A sample completed form (Figure 4.5) is provided to illustrate its use.

ANALYSIS FORM: SIMILARITIES AND DIFFERENCES

Today I am reading: _____

(Name of story, chapter, or article)

I am going to compare that to: _____

SIMILARITIES	DIFFERENCES

Figure 4.4 Analysis Form

Today I am reading: <u>Matilda</u>

I am going to compare that to: <u>Pippi Longstocking</u>

SIMILARITIES	DIFFERENCES
Matilda and Pippi are both smart.	Pippi loves her family. Matilda does not.
Both are nice, at least Matilda is nice to people she likes.	Pippi does nice things for her family. Matilda always plays tricks on them, like when she put glue on her father's wig or chemicals in her mother's shampoo.
Both like to read.	Pippi stays with her family but Matilda moves away to live with Miss Honey.
Both find kind people outside of their families who help them.	

Figure 4.5 Complete Analysis Form

Prediction

The final analytical skill is prediction. Once the student knows what happened (comprehension) and how the text is similar to or different from other text (analysis), he can answer the question, What do you think will happen next? One of the best examples in children's literature that blends comprehension, analysis, and prediction is E. B. White's *The Trumpet of the Swan*. Each chapter ends with a notation in the diary of the narrator, and each diary entry ends with a question. Such a question replaces the soporific "And they lived happily ever after" with the challenging "What do you think will happen next?" Among my happiest memories as a parent are the leisurely moments at bedtime after the evening's chapter had been completed, while Brooks and James, my biggest E. B. White fans, would ponder the question, "What do you think will happen next?"

The response is more than creative fantasy. Prediction is an analytical skill in which the reader considers previous events and the pattern in those events, and develops a theory. Based on what we know about a character's behavior in the past, how might he or she behave in the future? The relationship between the setting, plot events, and the attributes of a character will allow the young reader to speculate about what might happen next. The pleasure children take in this type of speculation is evidenced in the number of series books for children. The popularity of contemporary series such as *Redwall, Harry Potter,* and *Animorphs,* as well as those of a bygone era, such as *The Hardy Boys* and *Nancy Drew,* attests to our interest in the question, What is going to happen next? This is the key to helping students get beyond the typical journalistic book report and on to the intellectual challenge of writing the next chapter of the book and speculating on future events. In doing so, the children demonstrate their ability to apply reasoning to the question and their understanding of the characters, events, and setting of the book.

CONCLUSION

Of all the possible reasons for writing, perhaps the one most important to parents is that encouraging our children to write will help them to become better readers. From the stories in the earliest days of elementary school to the complexities of science and social studies texts in the fourth and fifth grades, students need the opportunity for understanding that only written reflections will allow. Provided with the opportunity to write summaries, analyses, and predictions, students will gain the confidence to consider increasingly complex text and master multiple levels of meaning. Writing improves the child's engagement with the text. Writing gives parents vital information about their child's reading comprehension and thinking processes. The reading-writing connection, in other words, not only helps the child become a better reader, but helps parents fulfill our role as the most important teacher our children will ever have.

5 Writing for an Audience

"**WHAT ARE** you writing about?" I asked Alexandra, one of the enthusiastic nine-year-old students in the elementary school newspaper club for which I am the parent advisor.

"The rain forest," she said, without looking up.

"Who are you writing it for?" I inquired.

With the withering look that is not uncommon when wise children are dealing with clueless adults, Alexandra responded, "For *me*."

Alexandra is a bright and capable student, a creative child, and a diligent writer. She can make qualitative distinctions when she reviews the writing of her peers and can identify with clarity and gentleness her friends' writing that is great, good, and in need of improvement. Moreover, Alexandra understands that occasionally one does write for someone else, such as when the teacher requires an assignment or when her mother suggests a thank-you note. But her response to "Who are you writing for?" reveals that Alexandra has not yet mastered the concept of audience.

In the first chapter, we explored several answers to the question Why write?

- Reading comprehension is enhanced through written summaries and analyses;
- Writing improves student performance in other academic areas, including social studies, science, and mathematics;
- Writing contributes to the creation of a sense of connection and personal efficacy by participation in society; and of course,
- Writing improves through practice, evaluation, editing, and rewriting.

Of those four reasons to write, none addresses Alexandra's dilemma. She understands, better than a good number of adults I know, the connections between reading and writing as well as the more subtle connections between writing and mathematics, science, and social studies. As a result of her work on the newspaper, she is even beginning to understand that her writing can influence others, including the opinions of her peers and the decisions of those in authority. Despite her intellectual assent to these rational reasons to write, Alexandra is unmoved in her fundamental conviction that when all is said and done, she is writing for herself. That is the dilemma that parents and teachers must resolve. On the one hand, there is extraordinary power in writing "for me": internal drive, satisfaction, and sustained reinforcement that psychologists refer to as intrinsic motivation. On the other hand, we know that writing—along with thinking, reasoning, and communication—will improve only as the result of a continued interaction between writer and reader. The mere presence of an audience can lend clarity to student writing that otherwise could be aimless and unfocused. When we add to that process the interaction with an audience, including questions, challenges, and subsequent revisions, then writing can improve from self-indulgent to sublime. As much as we value Alexandra's nine-year-old conception of herself as the ultimate reader of her work, we give her an extraordinary gift when we introduce to her the concept of audience.

WHAT DO AUDIENCES DO?

I hope that you were lucky enough to be the audience for your child's first steps and first words. How did you respond? With polite applause and a mixed review in the local newspaper? No. You cheered. You gushed. You offered wild applause. You hugged. You celebrated. Inevitably, the first steps were followed by an ungraceful landing; the first words were followed by gibberish. I don't know of a single parent who then announced, "All that applause and enthusiasm? Forget about it. If you want praise from me, come back when you are a competent walker and talker."

Children become competent walkers and talkers, and your encouragement and enthusiasm—that is, your behavior as the audience for these developments—are an important part of that process. When was the last time you offered similar degrees of applause, cheers, and encouragement for a paragraph in a school notebook? You get the behavior that you encourage and reward, whether your rewards are obvious, in the form of applause and cheers, or subtle, in the form of attention, listening, and respect. Audiences matter.

THE ENDURING INFLUENCE OF AUDIENCE

As a child prodigy and later as a young adult, Wolfgang Amadeus Mozart wrote letters to family and friends that reflect his keen attention to audience behavior. There are entire passages in his symphonies that are repeated in subsequent movements because, during early performances, the audiences broke into spontaneous applause the first time the passage was played. Today's audiences, in other words, are listening to an encore that was encouraged with applause three centuries ago. There will be many times in your child's life when you will not be there to provide standing ovations and effusive praise. You could respond to that inevitable prospect by saying, "Toughen up, kid. You'd better get used to it." Or you could begin the process of building emotional resilience in your child by remembering each day that you are his most important audience and that your response today will go a long way in shaping your child's future behavior. Do you want to receive letters from your future college student? Cherish the letters you get from a third grader. Do you want your high school student to share a social studies assignment with you? Read with care and diligence the work of your fifth grader.

THE PERSONALIZATION OF AUDIENCE

When parents applaud, the composition of the audience is obvious. When children consider the concept of audience in writing, however, the matter is less clear. In Alexandra's case, it is not that she fails to recognize that other people might read her work, but she has not considered that they will be moved by it in the same way that she has been able to move audiences in the past through other performances. If we are to help Alexandra connect with her audience, then we must be more specific than saying that she is writing for her classmates or a group of nameless, faceless adults. There is a person to whom she is writing, and that person represents the audience.

In the case of the rain forest essay, Alexandra's writing displays a concern about the health of indigenous people and the damage to animal habitats caused by some mining operations in South America. As a child who loves people and animals, Alexandra takes her work seriously. She wants to do something, but without an audience, the focus of her writing will remain her own feelings of unease and empathy. Using the table in Figure 5.1, consider how different audiences might influence the content, scope, and passion of Alexandra's work.

AUDIENCE	PURPOSE	RESULT
Alexandra	Learn about the rain forest. Get my feelings on paper.	Satisfaction with learning, but frustration and sadness that there are people and animals who are hurt and nothing seems to be getting better.
Mom, Dad, Grandma, and Uncle Andy	Teach them about the rain forest. (I'm always surprised how little grown-ups seem to know about important stuff!)	They will appreciate my work—I like that. They might give me some books about the rain forest. Uncle Andy might give me another subscription to *Ranger Rick* magazine. Maybe they will try to do something for the animals and people in the rain forest.
Ms. Carlson, my teacher	See that I am a good writer.	Give me a good grade and some recognition. What next? I guess another assignment. If she sees how important this is, maybe she will let me learn more about this.
Ranger Rick, Discovery magazine, *Boston Globe for Kids, Weekly Reader*	Help other kids understand why the rain forest is important. Help them learn about animals and people who are in big trouble. Help them understand that the problems in the rain forest affect all of us.	Maybe other kids would talk with their parents and teachers. Maybe they would write letters. Maybe they would raise money for the World Wildlife Federation or other organizations that help in the rain forest.
The president of the United States	Even though he's not the president in South America, our president can still do something about this. He could share our technology and help people change the way that they do mining and stop hurting people and animals.	I'm just a kid. Will he read my letter? He might write back. He might even give my letter to other people in the government who can help. At least he will know that I care and that I'm going to vote someday.

Figure 5.1. Writing for an Audience

As Alexandra's conception of her audience becomes clearer, the content of her writing becomes richer, her passion becomes greater, and her sense of purpose is stronger. Her writing changes from description to exposition and persuasion. Her focus is transformed from reflection to advocacy. Her voice as a writer emerges when she can see the face of Uncle Andy, hear the approval of a teacher, hold the letter from the editor who reviewed her story, and read the letter from the president, who thanked her for sharing her ideas.

WRITING TO PLEASE, WRITING TO CHALLENGE

I have conveyed the impression thus far that the relationship between writer and audience is a cordial one. The author seeks the favor of the audience, and when this feat has been performed successfully, the audience responds with approval. But what about those cases when the author intends to challenge, provoke, or disturb the audience? One of the most difficult things for authors of any age to accept is that writing that moves people will not always generate approval. If she persists in her writing about the rain forest, Alexandra may encounter reactions that are hostile or dismissive. Even in school, there will be times when she pours her heart into an essay and her very busy teacher responds with only a grade and perhaps a few words: "Very good." Parental interest and enthusiasm for the young writer's work can act as a hedge against the indifference or disapproval. Parents must always pay explicit and continuous attention to their children's writing. They must not only read it, but think about it, ask questions about it, encourage it, and learn from it. They must not offer reflexive, meaningless praise or incessant criticism but rather appreciation, support, and encouragement.

6 Brainstorming: First Steps for Reluctant Students

"**H**AVE YOU FINISHED your homework?" asked Julia.

"I can't think of anything to write about!" complained Heather.

"Oh, honey, I'm sure that you can think of something. Now go back and finish your homework."

"I told you—I can't *think* of anything!" And with that, Heather broke the pencil, crumpled her paper, and stomped out of the room.

Before this confrontation further escalates, let us take Heather's statement at face value. Surely she can think. The very fact that she is frustrated and angry is evidence that Heather understands the discrepancy between what she wishes she could do and what she is doing now. In fact, the problem certainly is not her inability to think, but rather that she is overwhelmed by the many possibilities. She is not able—not yet, at least—to convert the jumble of possibilities into a coherent plan for writing. Brainstorming, when done well, transforms Heather's challenge from a problem into an advantage. She will become the master of her ideas rather than the victim of intellectual paralysis. She will be happily surprised at her creativity. She will finish her homework. She may even get along better with her mother.

 WHAT IS BRAINSTORMING?

When a word is used frequently and in many different ways, it can take on widely different definitions and connotations. This is the case with brainstorming, where commonly held descriptions of the process range from an aimless and unproductive waste of time to a constructive process for expressing and organizing ideas. The confusion is understandable, considering these widely varying dictionary definitions:

> brainstorm n 1. *a series of sudden, violent cerebral disturbances* 2. *{Colloq.} a sudden inspiration, idea or plan.*

> —*Webster's New World Dictionary*, Second College Edition, p. 171

Here is another definition, provided by one of the third-grade students whose work will be used in this book to illustrate the writing process. James explained: "Brainstorming is the listing of ideas of your story. It's thinking up what's going to happen, and then you write it down. Sometimes I put the subject inside of a big circle, and then there are other circles all around the page that tell details of what's in the big circle."

I find James's definition a useful amplification of Webster's. It shows a clear understanding that brainstorming in the context of writing is neither sudden nor the result of inspiration, but rather is part of a deliberate process that requires time and energy. While a stickler for labels might suggest that the circle technique James uses is correctly described as a "web" and should be deferred until the completion of the brainstorming process, my experience is that children are not always as linear as adults would like them to be. Moreover, there is a subtle complexity to James's conception of brainstorming that involves both the power of free association and the intellectual discipline of discovering the interrelationships among ideas. By the end of such a process, he will probably have more than enough information for one story or essay and will be able to proceed to other pre-writing strategies with less reluctance.

WHAT'S THE BIG IDEA?

If Heather had the opportunity to react to James's definition of brainstorming, she might interrupt, "All those little circles are great for you, but I still don't get what goes in the big circle. I still can't think of anything to write about!" Instructing Heather to think harder or brainstorm with greater intensity will yield only frustration. We need to give her tools that will make the success of her brainstorming less dependent upon inspiration and more related to the strategies she employs. Four quick ways to get to the "big idea" employ lists, exaggeration, action, and pictures. The acronym LEAP will help you to remember these quick ways to help your child brainstorm.

Lists

Examples of effective lists include:

Things that I love
My favorite foods
Scary animals
Things I know a lot about
Things adults say too often
My favorite books

Exaggeration

The technique of exaggeration is a way to transform the ordinary into the ridiculous and, as a result, inspire new ways of thinking about people, events, and scenes. In response to the complaint that a subject is too boring, we can ask questions that encourage a different perspective through exaggeration. For example:

What would it feel like if you were as tall as a house?
What would you do if you could swim across the ocean?
How would people treat you if you had eight arms?
What would life be like if we lived in the ocean? On the moon?
What would you remember if you lived to be two hundred years old?
What if you could read people's minds?
What would animals say if they could talk to you?

Action

By adding action to ideas, people, or things, the writer can make associations that are not obvious. Brainstorming about actions can take several forms, including sequence, direction, and speed. In thinking about sequence, the writer asks, What will happen next? In thinking about direction, the writer can experiment with ideas about changes in direction by asking, What would happen if this character did things backwards? Brainstorms about speed allow the writer to accelerate or slow the action. Slowing down the action is a particularly helpful thought process. It allows us to notice minute details that might otherwise be lost in the fast pace of a narrative.

Pictures

For young writers, visual images can be much more compelling than words. A brainstorming session that starts with a vivid picture can yield a number of ideas that can become the subjects of future stories and essays. The pictures can be literal representations, such as pictures of family members or scenes from a school, park, or other familiar public place, or they can be abstract images, such as a contemporary painting or a piece of finger painting created by another child.

These four ideas—lists, exaggeration, action, and pictures—are just the beginning of methods to help your child brainstorm subjects for writing. Perhaps your child will resonate to a walk around the block, a folk ballad, a story from the childhood of a parent or grandparent, a nursery rhyme, a movement from a great symphony, or just some quiet time alone. One exceptionally creative young writer I know invents his best stories when he retreats to his room, arranges all of his stuffed animals in a pile before him, and assigns roles to each. He throws the animals in the air, gives them voices, characters, and actions, and within fifteen to twenty minutes, develops a fanciful and detailed story. With careful observation, you will find the brainstorming technique that is most successful for your child. Once you discover how to open the door to your child's creativity, you'll want to record those flashes of brilliance.

IDEA JOURNAL AND IDEA WALL

Brainstorming can be done without the immediate purpose of completing a writing assignment. The students in our newspaper club carry an "idea journal" with them every day. Sometimes they take their idea journals to recess, on field trips, or in the car with a parent while running errands. Events, people, and scenes that may appear mundane to an adult can spark the enthusiasm of a student writer. Moreover, observation is a skill that improves with practice. Your children will notice more things as they are more conscious and consistent in their observations. They will amplify their observations with feelings as they associate anger, sadness, empathy, and joy with the characters and events in their idea journal. Ultimately, they will add more details, notice similarities and differences, and have in their own handwriting the source of many ideas for stories and essays. When our oldest son, Brooks, was in second grade, we whitewashed one wall of the basement and announced that he and his friends could write anything—stories, pictures, cartoons, or just doodles—on it. "You mean it's okay to write on the wall?" he asked with more than a hint of skepticism. With our assurance that this was perfectly fine, he began to cover the wall and has not stopped his enthusiasm for writing since. The wall became a visible idea factory, covered with stories, pictures, lists, and ideas.

REDUCING STRESS FOR RELUCTANT WRITERS

The pressure to sit down and write can transform a normally energetic and creative child into one who is withdrawn, morose, and angry. By discovering brainstorming techniques that help a child break the logjam of ideas, you not only will help build creativity, but you will also help reduce stress and anxiety. These two objectives are closely related. One of the surest ways to inhibit creativity is to descend into the stress-filled dynamic of, "I've just got to think of something or I'm a failure!" When children are comfortable with different brainstorming techniques, they can confidently display their creativity at any time. The successful application of brainstorming techniques is not limited to creative writing. The analytical associations generated by exaggeration and action, for example, will improve the writer's descriptive skills. When students develop proficiency in creating lists, they will more easily break complex ideas into their component parts. When children can harness a stressful situation by turning it into a game, they can gain insight into maintaining control of their emotions. By separating the fun of brainstorming from academic chores, students can develop a skill that will serve them for a lifetime.

Pre-Writing: Organizing Ideas

YEARS AGO, I had a secretary who was endowed with remarkable candor. "I can always tell when you dictate a letter while you are driving on the highway and when you dictate one in the office," she said.

"What's the difference?" I asked.

"In the office, you think, plan, and then write. When you are driving, the letters are twice as long and say half as much."

The truth hurts. For some writers, the prospect of organizing their ideas before writing is as appealing as organizing their sock drawer. Once struck by the muse, they want to write. In the next few pages, you will learn how to help your child make the transition from brainstorming, where structure is optional and ideas flow like white-water rapids, to pre-writing, where organization and clarity will draw order from the chaos. The rapids are tamed into a gently flowing stream, where there are twists and turns, to be sure, but there is a clear beginning, middle, and end.

WORKING FROM THE "INSIDE-OUT"

When we look at a completed jigsaw puzzle, we are more likely to focus on the picture rather than the pieces. Yet when we solve a puzzle, we are forced to examine the individual pieces, fit them together, and work from the inside out. At the beginning of that process, we may not even know what the final picture will be. We see only how some pieces fit together and others do not. We might begin by grouping the pieces that

are alike in color or pattern. From those associations, we will find smaller characteristics, such as the shape of the individual pieces, and use those observations to fit two, then three, then a dozen pieces together. We must build the picture piece by piece.

The same is true when children solve the puzzle of working a jumble of ideas into a coherent piece of writing. The completed picture may not be clear yet, but they can work with what they have—the puzzle pieces produced during a brainstorming session or collected in an idea journal, and their understanding of how those pieces fit together. While the entire story may not be clear, the function of each piece usually is: Some pieces describe characters, others describe the setting, and yet others provide details about the plot. Although the persuasive essay is not yet in coherent form, some quotations, examples, and ideas support one side of an argument, and other evidence supports the other side. Whatever the type of writing, children can begin to group similar pieces of the puzzle together. Sometimes this process is a visual one, employing a graphic organizer (Figures 7.1a to 7.6a); other times, the organizational scheme involves an outline (see chapter 14). In either case, pre-writing is an absolutely essential step, whether the student is in third grade writing a story, in eighth grade writing an essay for a state test, or in college writing a final exam. Organization is a requirement for good writing, and pre-writing is the best way to ensure that one's writing is organized in a logical and coherent manner.

GRAPHIC ORGANIZERS

Your child's idea journal or brainstorming efforts may provide words and sentence fragments in a random order and without a clear method of organization. Graphic organizers will relate causes to effects, parts to the whole, and, as Napoleon said of his artillery, bring order to what would otherwise be a messy affair. There are six common types of graphic organizers.

Descriptive Pattern

The most common graphic organizer for younger elementary students is the Descriptive Pattern. It contains the main idea, such as the person, object, concept, or place to be described, in a large circle in the center. The surrounding circles provide details associated with the main idea in the center. (See Figures 7.1a and 7.1b.)

Sequence Patterns

Sequence Patterns are useful for fictional narratives and historical accounts. A key to effective reading comprehension is the ability to summarize the details of a story, including the ability to retell the sequence of events in order. When groups of students work on the creation of a Sequence Pattern, they might insert details at different places, starting with the ending that was clear in their minds, then going back to the beginning and slowly filling in the details as they collectively recall the events and sequence. Another use of the Sequence Pattern organizer is in conferences with writers. The pattern can display the events as the writer has created them in a first draft, and the listener can ask, "I see that you have these two events next to each other, but I don't understand how the first event led to the second event. Were there other things that happened that would help the reader understand? Could we insert some additional information between these two lines on the Sequence Pattern and then add those new details in your next draft of the story?" (See Figures 7.2a and 7.2b.)

Process/Cause Pattern

This pattern is useful for analytical essays, particularly in science and social studies. We might know the end event, represented in the box to the right. For example, we know that the water evaporated or that World War II started. But what were the events that led to the final effect? In the circles to the left of the box, students can enter proposed causes. Some of those causes might have additional causes, and thus the circles can branch off into "causes of causes." Because a single effect usually has multiple causes, the Process/Cause Pattern is also an excellent critical thinking exercise for students who want to think more deeply about an event in science or social studies. There is more to evaporation, for example, than "The sun dried up the water," and there is more to the origins of World War II than "The Japanese attacked Pearl Harbor." (See Figures 7.3a and 7.3b.)

Problem-Solution Pattern

This pattern helps the writer to consider alternative solutions for each problem by encouraging her to identify and compare different solutions before coming to a conclusion. This is particularly helpful in persuasive writing. Although the student may begin the paper with a strong conviction that there is only one clear solution to the problem, good persuasive writing requires more than the announcement of a conclusion. The reader must understand why one particular solution is the best alternative, and therefore the other alternatives must be noted and analyzed. (See Figures 7.4a and 7.4b.)

Generalization Pattern

This approach allows the writer to test the statement that, if true, should apply to many different circumstances. This is useful not only in analytical essays, but also in introspective writing. Children will characterize themselves as "no good in math" or complain that they "don't have any friends." The generalization can appear at the top, and then the rectangles below will include statements that may or may not be consistent with the generalization. If the statements are inconsistent ("I helped make dinner last night and measured all the ingredients exactly right") with the generalization ("I'm not good in math"), then one of the two statements is false and must be modified. (See Figures 7.5a and 7.5b.)

Concept Pattern

This is the most complex of the graphic organizers, though in practice it may be useful as a way to impose a basic organizational structure onto what otherwise would be the seemingly unrelated products of brainstorming. In its most elegant form, the Concept Pattern is like a visual outline, with each set of circles containing major subtopics that share a common relationship to the central theme contained in the large circle at the top. In practice, however, the Concept Pattern is likely to be a way of gathering many different ideas, facts, and illustrations into a coherent pattern. If a student is stuck in creating an outline, then the Concept Pattern might be a good way to break through the intellectual logjam, get some related ideas down on paper, see how some ideas and examples stick together in a logical relationship and how others belong in a different part of the structure. After the creation of the Concept Pattern, students can then move to the outline. (See Figures 7.6a and 7.6b.)

Other graphic organizers can be used, including those associated with computer flow charting, to show decision processes and sequences of events. The shapes and sizes of the elements of each organizer are not as important as the principle that thoughts on paper are much easier to organize and share than thoughts that reside only in the imagination of the writer. If a student is holding a pencil, squinting in concentration, and growing increasingly frustrated, then graphic organizers can be an excellent way to help make a small move in the right direction and reduce the writer's stress and anxiety.

Graphic Organizers in Action: A Case Study

James wanted to write a science report about sound. This might have something to do with the proximity of his bedroom to a teenage brother who plays the electric guitar at ear-splitting volume or his own interest in the cello. Without the use of pre-writing, James produced a fairly typical example of third-grade writing (Figure 7.8) that shows what he could remember, in the order in which he remembered it, about sound. Then he completed a web (Figure 7.9) in about ten minutes. A web is one of the simplest organizers, with a large circle in the middle representing the main idea. Surrounding the large circle are a series of smaller circles, each containing supporting ideas that are related to the main theme of the story or essay. Based on that document—and equipped with the same knowledge and understanding that he had when he wrote his first hasty essay—he produced another draft (Figure 7.10). The impact of organizational strategies on James's writing is dramatic. The remarkable contrast between the second draft and the first is not the result of more instruction or a lesson about the physics of sound. It is not even the result of a lecture about the value of organization in written communication. The only difference is the use of a graphic organizer.

Using the web or other graphic organizers is a skill that develops with practice. Too frequently students proceed immediately from an idea to a story or essay, without taking the time to organize their thoughts. Some children will find this step a frustrating delay. "I know what I'm going to write," they will complain. "Why should I waste time with a web?" If your child is an enthusiastic writer and wants to proceed immediately to a first draft, then you may waive the graphic organizer. However, it is absolutely essential that you agree on the principle "Your first draft is never your last draft." In the example of the "sound" essays, the first draft was spontaneously created without pre-writing. After you review your child's first draft, then you can ask questions, show your genuine interest in learning more, and introduce a graphic organizer to help your child prepare a second draft with more details and a more coherent structure. Over time, children will want to use pre-writing techniques even when a teacher does not require them. As they gain confidence in the use of these valuable tools, they realize that organizing their writing saves time and creates a superior essay or story.

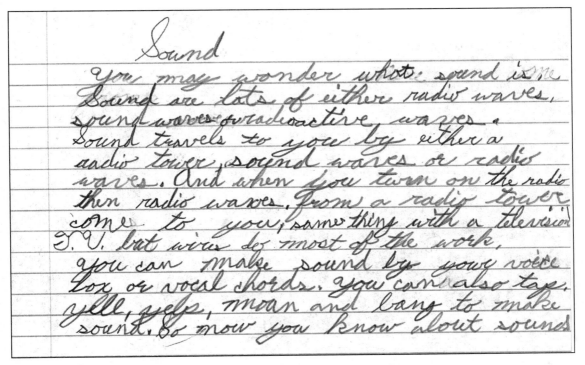

Figure 7.8. James's First Draft on Sound

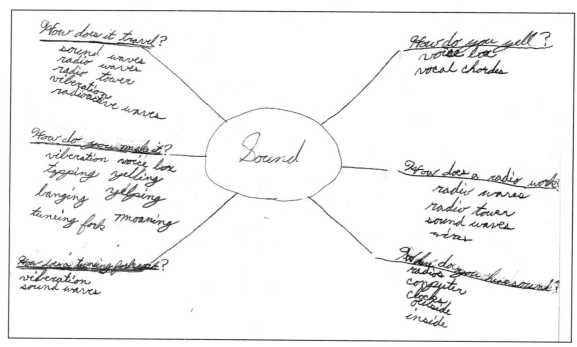

Figure 7.9. James's Descriptive Pattern Web on Sound

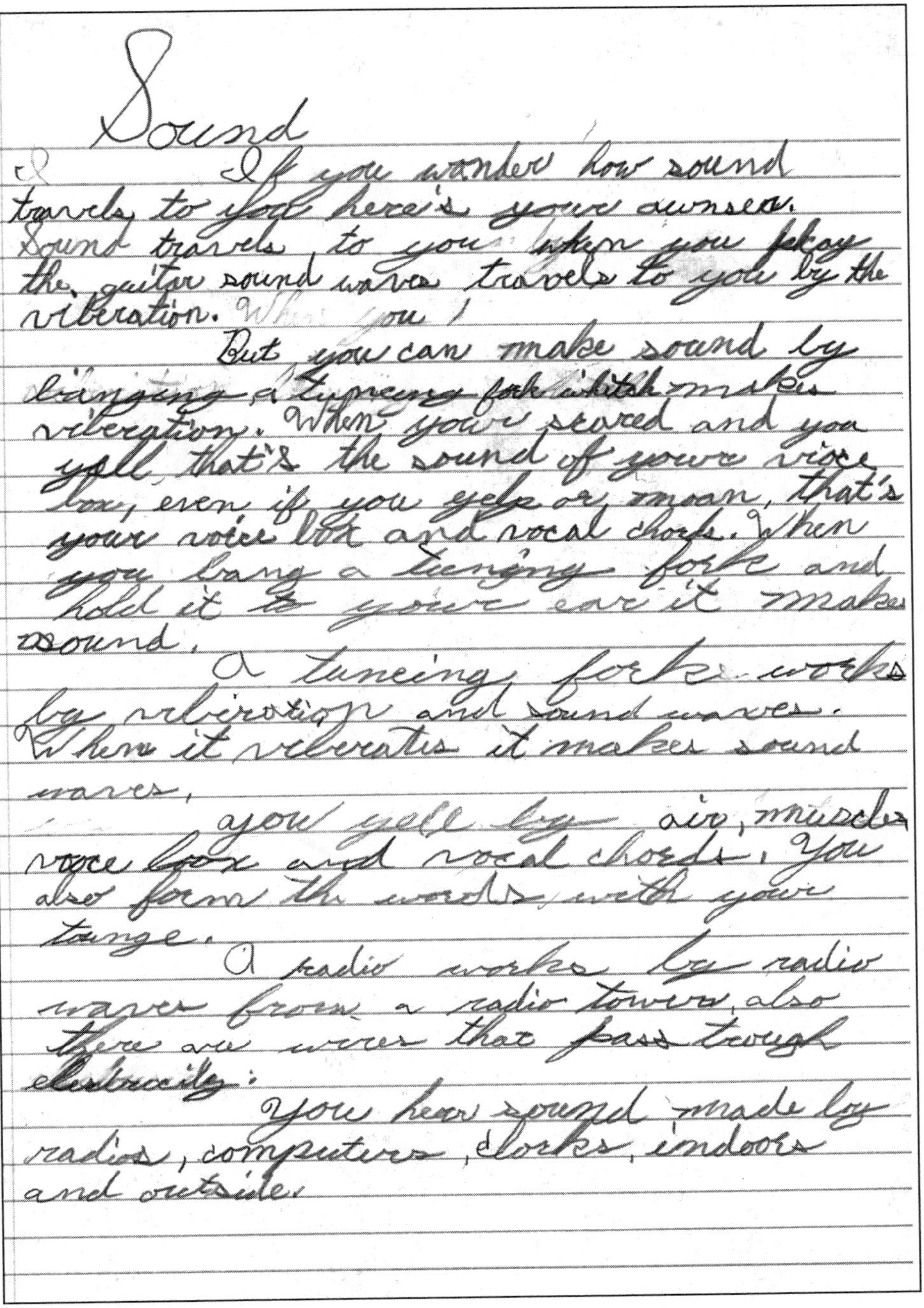

Sound

If you wonder how sound travels to you here's your answer. Sound travels to you when you pkay the guitar sound waves travels to you by the viberation. When you !

But you can make sound by banging a tuneing fork which makes viberation. When your scared and you yell, that's the sound of your voice box, even if you yelp or moan, that's your voice box and vocal chords. When you bang a tuneing forke and hold it to your ear it makes sound.

A tuneing forke works by viberation and sound waves. When it viberates it makes sound waves.

You yell by air, muscle voice box and vocal chords. You also form the words with your tunge.

A radio works by radio waves from a radio tower, also there are wires that pass trough electracity.

You hear sound made by radios, computers, clorks, indoors and outside.

Figure 7.10. James's Second Draft on Sound

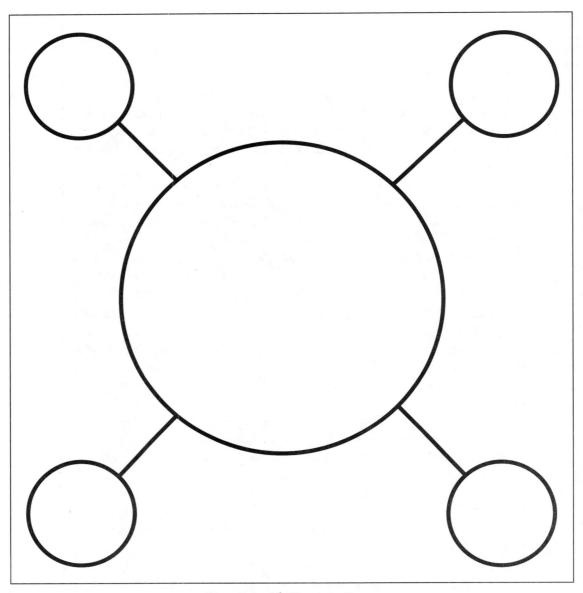

Figure 7.1a. The Descriptive Pattern

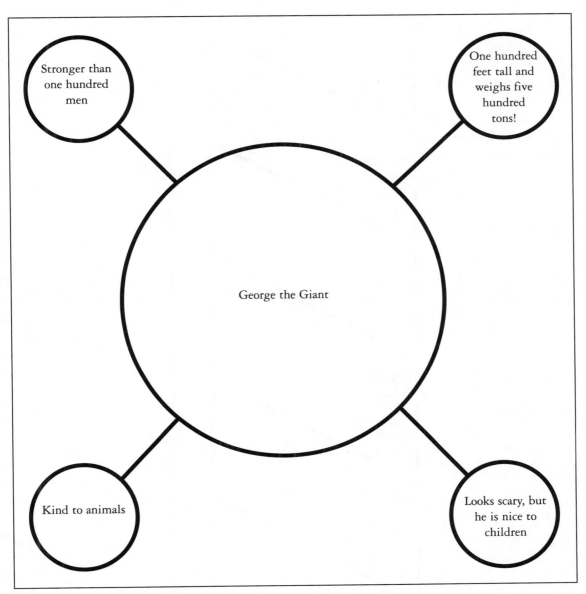

Figure 7.1b. My Story About George the Giant

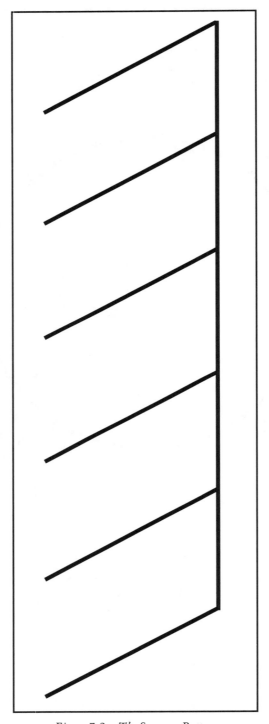

Figure 7.2a. The Sequence Pattern

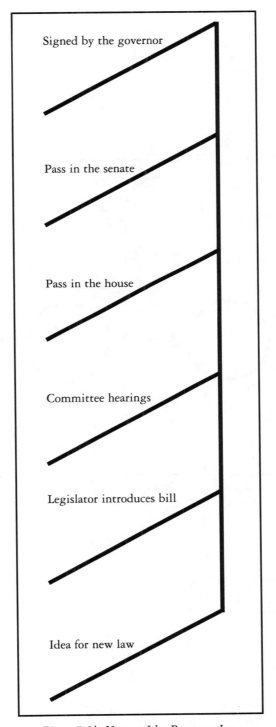

Figure 7.2b. How an Idea Becomes a Law

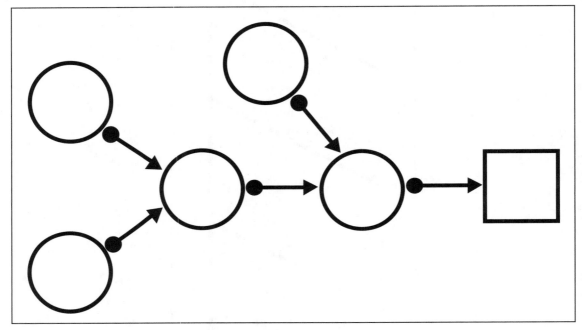

Figure 7.3a. The Process/Cause Pattern

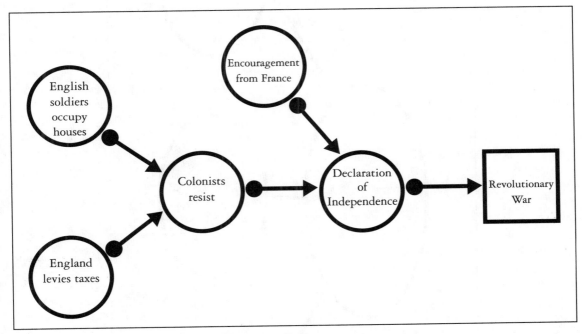

Figure 7.3b. What Caused the American Revolution?

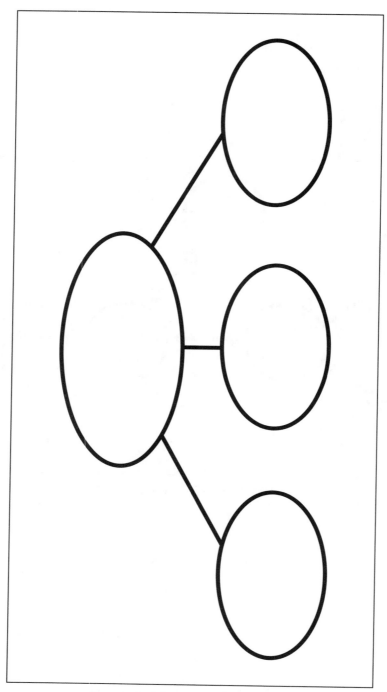

Figure 7.4a. The Problem-Solution Pattern

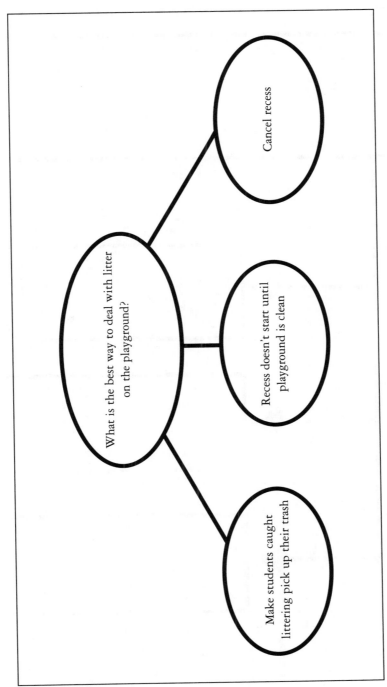

Figure 7.4b. Litter on the Playground

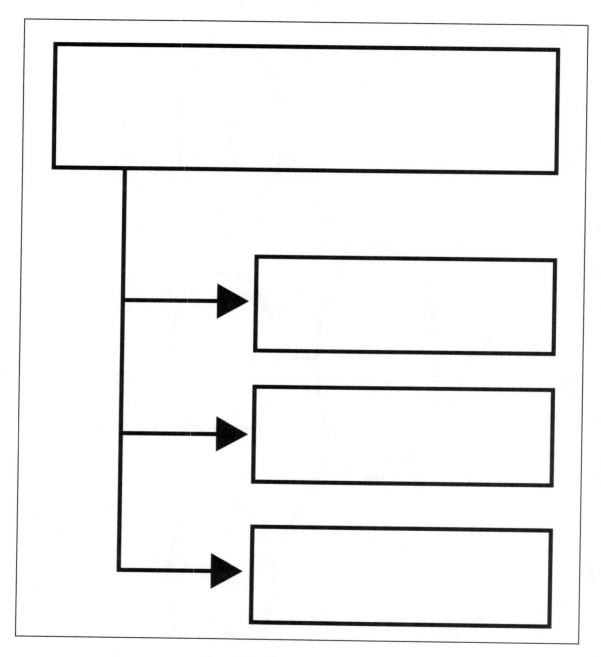

Figure 7.5a. The Generalization Pattern

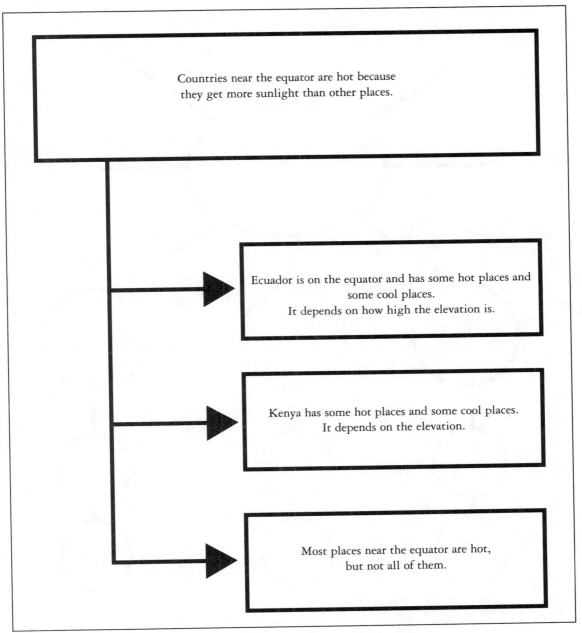

Countries near the equator are hot because
they get more sunlight than other places.

Ecuador is on the equator and has some hot places and
some cool places.
It depends on how high the elevation is.

Kenya has some hot places and some cool places.
It depends on the elevation.

Most places near the equator are hot,
but not all of them.

Figure 7.5b. Countries Near the Equator are Hot

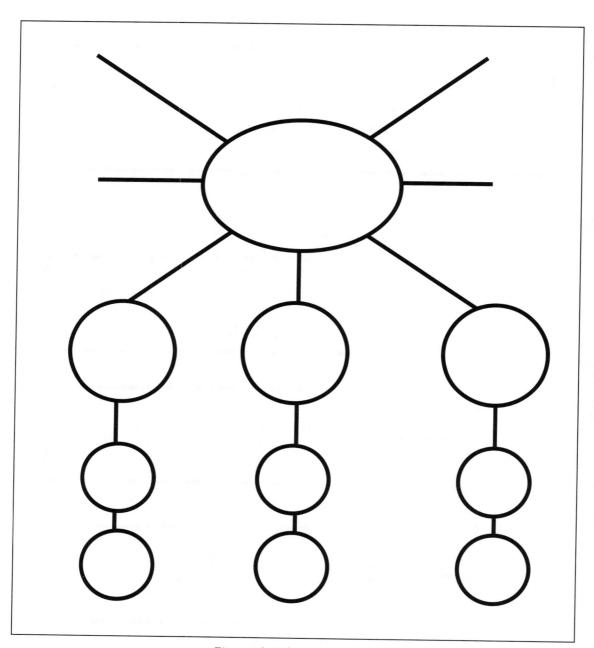

Figure 7.6a. The Concept Pattern

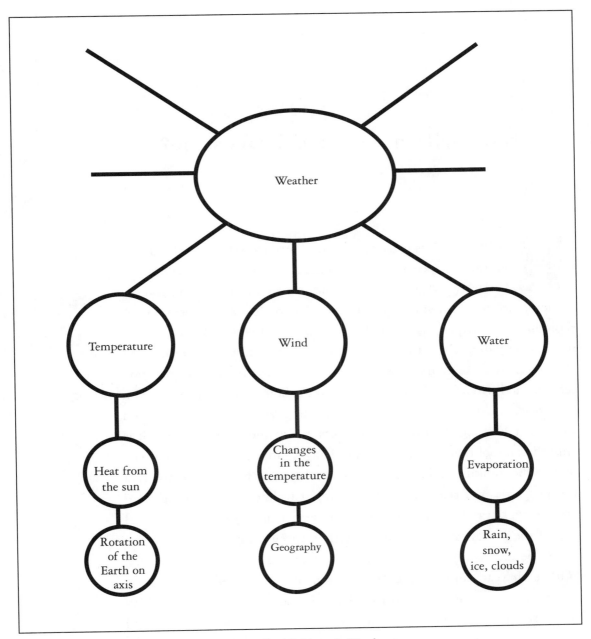

Figure 7.6b. All About the Weather

8   Handwriting or Word Processing?

"**HANDWRITING** is irrelevant!" proclaimed the self-assured technology expert, speaking to an audience of thousands of educators. "In a few years, the only pen that students will hold will contain a microprocessor with voice-recognition software. They will dictate their thoughts into the pen, which will then make a wireless transmission to a nearby computer, where the printed text will appear on the screen." The speaker is right, of course, about the improvements in voice-recognition software and wireless technology. He is wrong, however, about the wisdom of displacing handwriting with word processing. Although parents should welcome technology as a tool for students, we should remember that it is only that: a tool that performs tasks quickly. Computers do not, however, replace the thinking and creativity that are distinctly human. The thesis of this chapter is not that parents should reject technology, including word processing, but rather that they should preserve handwriting as an integral part of the processes of thinking, reflection, and writing.

To be sure, computers are alluring for students, teachers, and parents. With each year, computers become faster, more powerful, and cheaper. Technology is omnipresent in the classroom, and students acquire keyboard skills in preschool. Assignments that are completed on a word processor are easier for teachers to read, easier for students to revise, and, once they are saved on the school network or home hard drive, far less likely to be eaten by the family dog. More than fourteen million student essays are graded each year by an automated process that compares each student's paper to hundreds of hand-scored essays and instantly renders a grade very similar to what a teacher might have done after half an hour of work. An increase in high-stakes writing tests coupled with a national shortage of qualified teachers means an increased demand for the automated scoring of student papers. So, yes, students must have word processing skills. However, those who predict the demise of writing implements and the irrelevance of paper are wrong. They argue that books, pencils, and paper are, after all, just *so* twentieth century. The same experts, however, do not seem to notice that even as computer hardware, software, and the number of people with the skills to use them have exploded, the number of books published has increased, not diminished. Moreover, the technological revolution of the past two decades has not reduced the impact of the handwritten note of thanks to a grandparent, the carefully crafted love letter left on a pillow, or the note of sympathy gently handed to a grieving friend. Words have power not only in their meaning but in their physical presence on the page and physical connection with the person who wrote them.

WRITING IS MORE THAN LETTERS ON A PAGE

One can accept the value of technology without rendering the physical acts of holding a book or pressing a pen irrelevant. If writing were the mere act of crafting letters, then it might make sense that the more quickly and neatly one can form the letters, the better one can write. By that standard, word processing is the clear victor. But even the most proficient fourth-grade keyboarder knows that writing is more than assembling letters quickly and neatly. Writing is about thinking, reflecting, creating, pausing, and thinking some more. Writing is a process, not a product. Of course, this uneven and necessarily interrupted process can be accomplished with a computer, and I am not making a case against word processors. However, I am emphatically making the case that parents should not dismiss their children's need to take pen or pencil in hand and write clearly and neatly. It is not merely the act of committing words to paper that has value. The multiple processes involved in editing, revising, and reflecting are equally as valuable. While it is true that editing can take place on a word processor, children will better hone their skills by striking out unnecessary words, adding details, and making visible handwritten changes in their papers.

YOUNG CHILDREN AND WORD PROCESSORS

Because children now acquire keyboarding skills so early, it may seem logical that they use sophisticated word processing software. In fact, however, parents of elementary students can ensure that their children get the optimum educational benefit from using word processors by following these guidelines:

Turn the automatic spell checker and grammar checker off.

Some of the most common student errors are not corrected by a computerized spell checker, and thus the contention that "I checked the spelling" is simply untrue in a paper in which "it's" is improperly substituted for "its" and "their" inaccurately replaces "there" or "they're." Moreover, because children spell phonetically, the computer "correction" to the spelling entered by the child may result in an entirely different word than the writer had intended. For example, when students recently wrote an essay for Veterans Day, one child's helpful word processing program replaced "Mureen" (her grandfather had served in the United States Marine Corps) with "Maureen." This seemed the best choice to the child, as the other possible computer-suggested replacements were "Tureen," "Murrain," "Murex," and "Uren." Despite the computer's assurance that the essay contained flawless spelling, the student was assured by her grandmother that Grandpa had not served in the Maureen Corps during the war. Similarly, grammar checkers are known for making suggested changes that are either incorrect within the context of the piece or absurd.

Use large fonts sizes, such as 14- to 16-point type.

When computer-generated print looks like a book, children are reluctant to edit it. Books and computers convey authority and permanence, but we want children to edit, reflect, and revise their work. Compare this example of third-grade writing to the typeface in this book.

To generate a paper that is comparable to the size with which a child is more familiar, we would need letters that are significantly larger.

✳ Use triple or quadruple spacing and wide margins through the third grade.

Although teachers beyond the third grade may be comfortable with traditional double-spaced format, teachers from kindergarten through the third grade typically need more space for comments, corrections, and notes to the student. If the text is too dense on the page, the student may be confronted with a sea of red ink and an unfortunate message of incompetence. Teachers know that corrections must be clear, gentle, and incremental, and those objectives for constructive help to students are far easier to achieve when there is abundant space on the page.

✳ Balance word processing with handwriting.

In the Stanley School newspaper club, which I advise, we use computers for final composition and publication. The publication is entirely written and edited by students in the third, fourth, and fifth grades. They create the initial drafts of every story by hand. First, students record lists, outlines, interview notes, and other comments in their "reporter's notebooks," which they carry on field trips, on the playground, and to the scene of every story they cover. From those raw notes, they create the first draft of their articles and confer with other club members as they revise and edit their work, still using pencil and paper. The very act of crossing out and revising words, playing with language, responding to inquiries from fellow students, and maintaining a physical record of the power of revision gives these students more powerful writing skills than had they simply dictated their initial thoughts into the end of an electronic pen and let the computer do the rest of the work. The students in the newspaper club are expert computer users. They not only use word processing programs, but also use programs that create graphs, tables, charts, pictures, and multiple-column formats. However, their sophistication in the use of technology does not diminish the usefulness of their handwritten notes in their reporter's notebooks or their handwritten drafts and collaborative work to improve their writing.

CURSIVE OR PRINTING?

Evidence clearly demonstrates that writing is one of the most important academic skills your child can develop. Although my children and my students make extensive use of technology, I am also convinced that handwriting is an important part of the writing process. If students would write more frequently, edit and revise their work, and collaborate with peers to improve their writing, they would be more successful in every academic discipline and gain lifelong social and intellectual skills. I cannot make the same claim for the use of cursive. Although I appreciate that my children have learned cursive, two of them write in a splendid script while the other two might as well use hieroglyphics. For the two children who have not mastered cursive (one of whom was the top graduate of his high school and a published author), I must decide which battles are worth fighting. It is essential that they write, just as it is imperative that they read, take challenging courses, live with integrity, and treat other people with dignity and respect. If they can do all of those things and print rather than use cursive in their handwritten communications, then I am a happy parent and teacher.

WHAT IF THE TEACHER INSISTS ON CURSIVE?

If the mechanics of writing cursive script become so laborious that students reduce the quantity and quality of their writing, then we have misplaced our priorities. Our children's ideas are important and powerful. The clarity and accuracy with which they express those ideas is an important part of effective written expression. But the choice of cursive or handwriting is about as significant as the choice of font style. Some people like Arial and others prefer Times New Roman. It is a secondary concern to our central focus on writing. If your child is struggling with cursive, consider a meeting with the teacher to discuss the priorities. Hallowed though the tradition of cursive writing may be, it's a good bet that thinking, reasoning, reading, and writing are all higher on the list of the teacher's priorities than font style. If you are an advocate for your child on matters such as this, then you have a great deal more influence when you maintain high expectations for reading challenging books and editing written work that requires revision.

How to Give Student Writers Encouraging Feedback

EVERY READER probably has a memory of a paper that was carefully crafted and submitted to a parent or a teacher with pride. We were crushed when the paper was returned without an acknowledgment of our creativity and hard work but with a red circle around every flaw. In that moment it seemed that our mistakes were all that mattered. Our motivation to succeed on the next paper was, at best, limited. At the other extreme, parents' and teachers' polite but vague "Good job!" was equally unhelpful. We may even have wondered if the person to whom we submitted our work had read it with care. We saw a smiley face—and nothing else—and wondered exactly what it was smiling about. Did it notice our new vocabulary? Our vivid descriptions? Our clever ending?

MOTIVATIONAL FEEDBACK: A CASE STUDY

In stark contrast to feedback that is artificially effusive or unproductively critical, there stands the example of Professor Hillier, an eminent Shakespearean scholar and full professor, who would take time each semester to teach composition to a group of first-year college students. When I received papers back from him, I wondered at first if he had read them, as there were only scattered pencil marks on the page. Then, turning to the final page, I would find a paragraph, sometimes a full page, of typewritten notes that gave his detailed reactions to my essay. Even when his remarks were critical—and they frequently were—I was elated by the astonishing care that he lavished on each sentence and paragraph. He gave each student a gift far greater in value than a smiley face; he demonstrated that he took us seriously. Similarly, parents give children encouragement and motivation through feedback that is specific, honest, accurate, and consistent. This is more challenging and time-consuming than the awarding of gold stars or incomprehensible assurances that "You can do better next time." Our labor will be rewarded. After all, our kids want to know, "How will I do better if you don't tell me?"

MYTHS ABOUT MOTIVATION

Until very recently, educators, psychologists, and parents embraced the belief that a vaguely defined quality called "self-esteem" was directly related to student achievement. This seemed to make sense. The circular reasoning was that since successful students were generally confident in their abilities and felt pretty good about themselves, it must follow that people who felt pretty good about themselves would become successful students. The challenge shifted from how to make kids become successful students to how to make kids feel good about themselves. During the 1990s I heard educators and school principals state with conviction that "the primary purpose of this school is to build the self-esteem of our students." In recent days I have heard parents extol the virtues of self-esteem as the most important part of their child's educational experience and as a decision-making condition by which activities are judged. "She likes the modeling class because it builds her self-esteem," they say. "We stopped piano lessons because it was hurting her self-esteem," they explain. Worst of all, parents and teachers assert, "I can't tell him that his paper wasn't satisfactory. That will hurt his self-esteem." With such logic, affirmation is more important than support for hard work, challenge to improve performance is oppressive, and truth is a threat to be avoided.

By embracing these myths, parents, teachers, and children delicately dance around the fact that children are not always wonderful and their work is not always proficient. Children know when adults are lying to them, yet we find it difficult to resist applauding effort for its own sake. If we are honest, we'll admit that we—parents, children, and teachers—have grown quite comfortable with these easygoing, feel-good exchanges. Thus, the dance continues until one day, a teacher, professor, colleague, or employer asks, "Who told you that this level of quality was satisfactory?" If our children are lucky, this unpleasant confrontation happens fairly early in their academic careers. Unfortunately, for legions of students the chasm between their opinion of the quality of their work and the truth is not revealed until college or their first job.

THE QUALITIES OF EFFECTIVE FEEDBACK

Consider what you already know about effective feedback. Your expertise in this matter comes from those areas in which you have already coached your child to achieve something that was difficult and perhaps seemed impossible. Three examples of childhood skills that were acquired in large part because of your expertise in effective feedback are walking, potty training, and taking turns. In each, your feedback was effective because it shared three characteristics: specificity, consistency, and accuracy. If you have coached your child in the acquisition of other skills, from kicking a soccer goal to the completion of the B-flat scale on the saxophone, to the finer points of sibling relationships without tears, then the same criteria for effective feedback apply.

Specificity

First, you were specific. There was no ambiguity about the difference between standing up and falling down or between hitting the potty and missing it. Close did not count; the goal was specific and clear. This degree of specificity stands in stark contrast to generalized praise and ambiguous criticism. We do not notice and applaud the intention to share and take turns, only the actual behavior. Even very young children know the difference between sharing the dump truck with their sister and displaying it to her with clenched fingers while maintaining unquestioned control of the toy.

Alli is a second-grade student who wrote about spring (Figure 9.1). Her penmanship is superb as is her capitalization and punctuation.

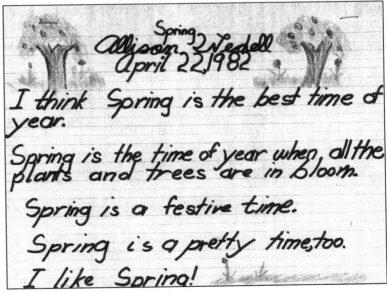

Figure 9.1

Alli's teacher then asked her to compare spring to another season. The result of that effort is in Figure 9.2. Once again, the legibility is excellent, but the ideas are not fully developed. Alli's mother provided feedback that was specific and encouraging. It is particularly noteworthy that Alli's mother asked questions, indicating her sincere interest and encouraging detailed elaboration in the next draft. The result is in Figure 9.3.

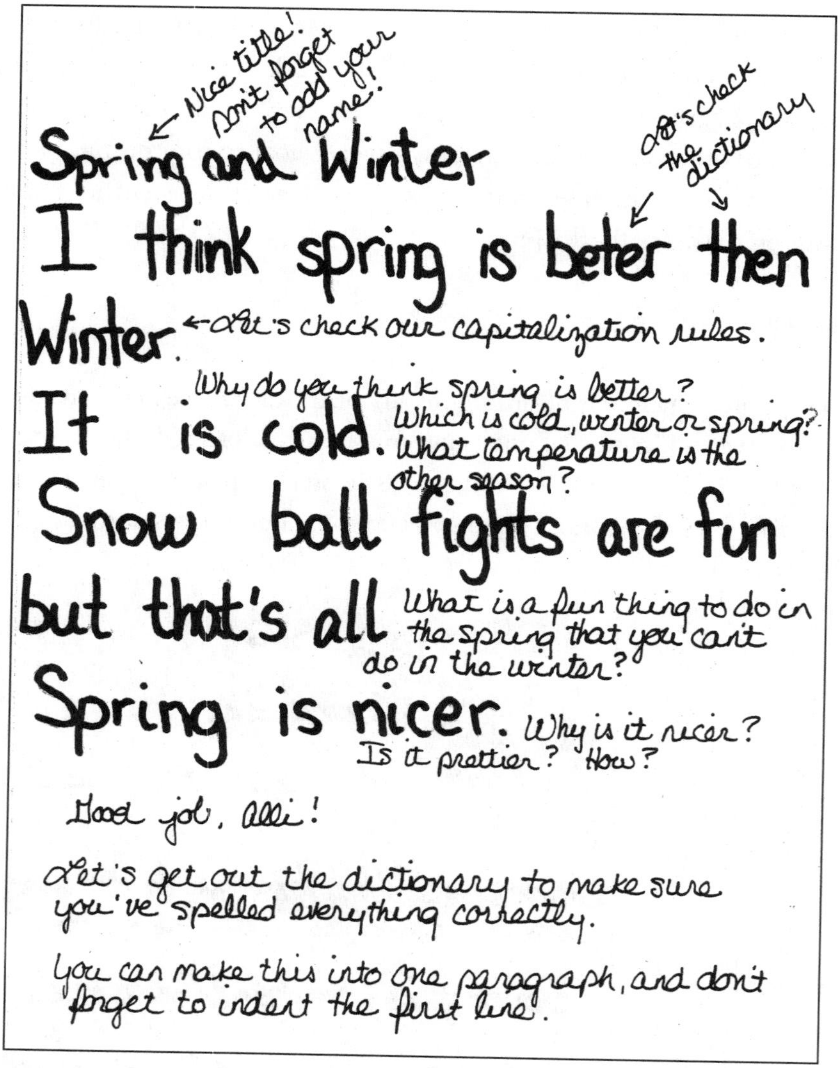
← Nice title! Don't forget to add your name!

Spring and Winter

Let's check the dictionary

I think spring is beter then Winter. ← Let's check our capitalization rules.

Why do you think spring is better?

It is cold. Which is cold, winter or spring? What temperature is the other season?

Snow ball fights are fun but that's all What is a fun thing to do in the spring that you can't do in the winter?

Spring is nicer. Why is it nicer? Is it prettier? How?

Good job, Alli!

Let's get out the dictionary to make sure you've spelled everything correctly.

You can make this into one paragraph, and don't forget to indent the first line.

Figure 9.2

```
┌─────────────────────────────────────────────────────┐
│  Spring and Winter          by Alli                   │
│                                                        │
│      I think spring is better than winter.  Winter is cold, but │
│                                                        │
│  spring is warm.  I would rather be warm than cold.  When I'm │
│                                                        │
│  cold, I shiver and my teeth chatter, but when I'm warm, it is │
│                                                        │
│  easier to have fun.  I think snowball fights are the only way to │
│                                                        │
│  have fun in the winter, but in the spring, there are lots of fun │
│                                                        │
│  things to do.  I can have picnics with my friends, and play │
│                                                        │
│  with my dog, and take long walks with my dad to look at the │
│                                                        │
│  blooming trees and flowers.  Green is my favorite color and │
│                                                        │
│  there is much more green in spring than in winter.  Those │
│                                                        │
│  are all the reasons I think spring is nicer than winter. │
└─────────────────────────────────────────────────────┘
```

Figure 9.3

❇Consistency

Second, you were consistent. You praised every step. Each instance of taking turns was noticed and appreciated. The same consistency is routinely used by parents who encourage
the development of new athletic, musical, or social skills. Saying "please" does not come
naturally to children any more than does kicking a football, playing the violin, or holding
the first position in ballet class. In each instance, however, parents provide consistent encouragement not only for the final display of skill, but for each incremental step along the

way. When it comes to student writing, parents can be overwhelmed by the girth of the weekly "parent packet" that frequently arrives on Friday afternoon somewhere near the bottom of the backpack. It is nevertheless important to take time to review each page of work and consistently praise the work that displays your child's successful efforts. Because effective feedback must be accurate, the review of school material requires some time. Not every paper is wonderful, and our children know this. Somewhere in that pile is a line or a paragraph that is worthy of special notice. If we are to provide consistent feedback, then we must take the time to find those gems and respond to them appropriately.

Accuracy

The third characteristic of your effective feedback is accuracy. In the context of academic performance, our children know when we are accurate in our feedback and when we are not. They know, or soon will discover, the difference between excellent writing and work that is barely satisfactory. Unfortunately, parents and teachers do not always provide a clear and specific way to analyze student work. Without a clear method of providing feedback to our children, we offer a general description when a more complex analysis is required. When our children are engaged in a complex task such as writing, we can no longer settle for broad feedback—it's "good" or it's not. We need a more sophisticated approach that will distinguish different qualities of writing and also provide a continuum of analysis for each quality. This method of feedback requires a device for differentiating four types of work from one another: work that is wonderful, work that is proficient, work that is very close but not quite there, and work that is far from the mark. Many educators refer to such a device as a rubric, but I prefer the term, "scoring guide."

SCORING GUIDES: THE KEY TO MEANINGFUL, ACCURATE, AND ENCOURAGING FEEDBACK

A scoring guide identifies the specific criteria that your child must satisfy in order to meet your local or state writing standards. Some teachers create scoring guides for each assignment, while other teachers apply a general scoring guide to every writing task. (Several examples of scoring rubrics used to grade state writing tests can be found in appendix B.) It is absolutely imperative that parents have a copy of whatever scoring guides are in use; you cannot help your child meet requirements if you do not have a clear idea of what those requirements are. The standards alone do not provide sufficient detail for coaching individual students, but a good scoring guide will provide clear detail about what quality is expected. Typically, scoring guides identify different levels of student performance, ranging from a very high level, such as "advanced" or "exemplary" to a low level such as "below basic" or "not meeting standards." In other cases, the scoring guides simply offer numerical labels, typically from 4 to 1 or 6 to 1, depending on the state.

The reason that scoring guides are so important for parents is that they allow you to give your child specific feedback that is directly related to the aspects of his writing on which others—his teacher, your state education department—will judge him. By carefully examining the criteria of the scoring guide, you will be able to identify where your child has excelled and where additional work is necessary. In addition, you can use the different levels of quality to coach your child along a continuum of performance. If your child is already proficient, then you can work on attaining the highest level of writing performance. If your child is just learning to master a paragraph, then you can coach her to acquire the skills to move to a "progressing" level, enjoy that accomplishment, and later on move to "proficient" and higher levels of performance. One of the most important functions of scoring guides is student self-evaluation. Before you provide extensive feedback to your child, ask her to carefully compare the requirements of the scoring guide to her own paper. Because children are frequently accustomed to receiving feedback only from teachers and parents, the practice of self-evaluation may seem unusual, but it is a vital skill. You will not be there for the state test or, for that matter, for the final exams in the secondary school and college years that lie ahead. It is essential that you nurture in your child the real confidence to objectively compare a set of performance criteria to a piece of work and to make appropriate corrections.

Scoring guides have two dimensions, including the various components of writing and the quality of each component. Consider a simple example (Table 9.1) that includes two components of writing: organization and conventions. By organization, we mean that the writer provided a clear and logical beginning, middle, and end. By conventions, we mean that the writer applied the rules of grammar, spelling, and punctuation correctly.

TABLE 9.1. SAMPLE SCORING GUIDE

	BASIC ("I'm working on it.")	PROGRESSING ("I'm almost there.")	PROFICIENT ("I did it!")	EXEMPLARY ("Knocked my socks off!")
Organization	The reader can't understand what the writer intends to say.	The topic sentence tells the reader what to expect, but there is not a clear beginning, middle, and end.	There is a clear beginning, middle, and end.	There is a clear beginning, middle, and end, with transitions between each section.
Conventions	The reader can't understand what the writer intends.	The spelling and punctuation mistakes sometimes prevent the reader from understanding what the writer intends.	There are a few mistakes, but they do not prevent the reader from understanding what the writer intends.	There are no errors in grammar, spelling, or punctuation.

Rather than saying, "Your writing was great!" or "This really needs work—look at all those mistakes!" a parent or teacher can meet the criteria for effective and encouraging feedback. We can be specific, consistent, and accurate. We might say, for example:

"I noticed that you had a beginning, middle, and end. That's great. It means that your writing was very organized, because in the first sentence I understood what the paragraph was about, in the middle you gave me some important details, and at the end, you let me know why all of those details were important to come to a conclusion. I also noticed that some of the sentences didn't start with a capital letter and that you probably guessed at some of the spelling. That's okay, but for your next draft, can you check the words that I underlined in the dictionary to make sure that your spelling is accurate? You already know about capitals at the beginning of a sentence, so I expect you to fix those mistakes on your own. The setting of your story and the characters are so interesting that I can't wait to see the next draft."

Because we read carefully and made judgments about all aspects of the writing, we can be honest and encouraging. The organization is fine, but the conventions need work. Because conventions are complex, we might be moving only from a basic to a progressing level on conventions. While the next draft will probably have better spelling and capitalization, there will be numerous errors in grammar and usage. That is a challenge for another day, when we are making the next qualitative leap from progressing to proficient performance. Most important, our child knows that we are not operating in the binary world of "okay" and "not okay" but in a complex continuum that moves slowly from performance that is far below what it should be to performance that is making progress, to proficiency, to exemplary work.

In the example provided in this chapter, the vertical dimension of the scoring guide includes only two elements, organization and conventions. As our children mature as writers, the number of elements we consider will grow in quantity and complexity. It is important, however, that we not overwhelm a child with demands that lead to frustration and resignation. Rather, we must provide reassurance, step by step, for achievements, clear expectations for the next level of performance, and specific direction for how to reach that objective.

ENCOURAGING THE DISCOURAGED AND CHALLENGING THE COMPLACENT

Parents face two challenges as they review their child's work. First, if parents are too critical, they risk discouraging a child who is already fearful of failure. Second, if they are unwilling to confront the difference between the present performance of their child and the next level of proficiency, they have counseled complacency for a child who needs to be challenged. Many parents can recall their own experiences as an exasperated novice or a proficient but complacent performer who needed a greater challenge. My own recent experience from both of these perspectives is revealing, not about my successes, but about the wisdom of my teachers.

Encouraging the Discouraged: A Case Study

In order to provide a sufficient degree of empathy with their frustrated children, I would recommend that parents become a novice at something. My decision to take up the cello in my late forties has provided a glimpse of what children must endure in school. On my first day of lessons, I raced to a strange building in a place far away from home, carrying a large and heavy burden. Then I arrived at the wrong room. Even after learning the geography of the building and despite my best planning and my initially positive attitude, I sank into my seat late, humiliated, and despairing that I had the competence to be there. The work that I had performed only hours before did not come out the way I had intended. And when my teacher attempted to reassure me about the things I did well, I saw only my obvious deficiencies. In other words, I felt very much like an elementary school student. My wonderful teacher, Reinmar Seidler, knows better than to rhapsodize that my performance is reminiscent of Yo-Yo Ma, because we both know that to be untrue. But he can say that on two or three measures my bow produced a more musical quality than the previous lesson, and that with a little different finger and elbow position in the left hand, my next performance will be even better. Neither the proficient nor exemplary levels of performance are accessible to me yet, but I am making progress that we can assess with specificity, consistency, and accuracy.

My cello teacher models the performance he wants, and then asks me to invent exercises that will help me move from where I am to where I wish to be. In this manner, he turns my errors into opportunities for success.

Allowing children to invent their own exercises is a fascinating technique. When applied in the context of writing, there are two excellent results. Children tend to be very specific and clear in their criteria for success, and they also set rigorous expectations for themselves. For example, I have seen second-grade students review a set of papers and then invent both the activity and the evaluation that they needed. Although the teacher may not have had time to create twenty-six different assignments, the children had no trouble identifying their needs as they created the exercise that reflected their greatest need:

"I need more details in my story, so I'll make a list of everything about Catherine [the heroine of the story]."

"I make terrible p's, q's, j's, and g's—I'm going to make a whole page of them."

"My reader didn't understand what happened in my story. I'm going to make a time line to show the order that things happened and then write the story again."

Just as some cello students need work on slurs and others need work moving from first to second position, some writing students need work on details, while others require focus on legibility and organization. Allowing children to create an assignment is a great way to empower them and engage their interest.

Challenging the Complacent: A Case Study

Scoring guides can encourage the discouraged student and challenge the complacent student. For this lesson, I am indebted to my piano teacher, the concert pianist and Harvard faculty member Ludmilla Lifson. Unlike my novice foray into the cello, I am an experienced pianist, used to Chopin, Debussy, and applause. Not so fast, Ms. Lifson reminds me. I can play the notes proficiently and become complacent, but to the ears of an experienced musician I am merely pressing the buttons. "There is just playing the notes," Ms. Lifson says, "and there is music." She helps me to find the inner voice in a Bach fugue and the mystery in a Chopin nocturne. In other words, she guides me on the difficult journey from performance that is proficient to the elusive one that is exemplary. In this way, she holds my interest, makes me reconsider my assumptions, challenges my complacency, and helps me to do my best work. There are many parents whose children are proficient. They were reading in kindergarten. They meet the expectations of their teachers and exceed the performance of their classmates. Yet their parents have the uncomfortable feeling that they should not settle for the academic equivalent of merely playing the notes. In order to guide their children to higher levels of performance and challenge their acceptance of proficient performance, parents must provide feedback with the same specificity, accuracy, and feedback.

Ms. Lifson does not command me to "be Rubinstein!" but gently and clearly shows me the difference between where I am and where I wish to be. She guides me to recordings of the masters, just as parents who want their children to improve their writing will guide their children to the literature of great writers. While great musicianship, like great writing, may appear to be mysterious, she knows that Edison's formulation for genius applies in this realm as well: "One percent inspiration, ninety-nine percent perspiration." Thus, Edison's numerous failures are less well recalled but were nonetheless essential antecedents to his successes. Hemingway's multiple drafts preceded *For Whom the Bell Tolls*. Great teachers in the rank of Reinmar Seidler and Ludmilla Lifson practice every day, placing themselves in the role of students. Their empathy as well as their skill informs their ability to serve as models for teachers and parents.

Parents need not be published authors to offer effective feedback on student writing any more than they need to be Olympic soccer players in order to coach their children in the sport. However, they must be specific, consistent, and accurate in their feedback.

THE ART OF FEEDBACK: THE RIGHT VOICE AT THE RIGHT TIME

Just as an adult can simultaneously be a struggling cellist and a proficient pianist, a child can be approaching expertise in the creation of narrative fiction while at the same time exhibiting the characteristics of a novice when writing an analytical essay. Because children can vary within moments across the performance continuum from novice to progressing to proficient to exemplary, parents and teachers must be ready to vary their feedback techniques appropriately. As a result, this chapter does not suggest a "one size fits all" approach to feedback. While the characteristics of effective feedback—specificity, consistency, and accuracy—remain the same, the methods of providing that feedback will vary from one situation to the next. These characteristics suggest the technique. The art, however, is in the balance between encouragement and challenge.

10 Writing Letters

"**IT'S FOR ME!**" shouted Hillary as she tore open the envelope. "Aunt Jean wrote to me again. It's the second letter this month. Can you believe it? I'm going to write her back right now." And with that, Hillary marched to her room and began another multipage letter describing the events of her day, her successes in field hockey, her newest best friend, the misbehavior of her brother, and the other details of her life. When copies of her report on the rain forest, a poem, and a short story were added to the package, Hillary's letter required extra postage.

It was not always so, particularly from a girl whose typical answer to her mother's inquiry about the day was an abrupt, "Nothing." When Hillary's mother initially suggested writing a letter to Aunt Jean, Hillary, incredulous, whined, "She didn't send me a present—why do I have to write to her?" But at her mother's insistence, Hillary penned a hasty note:

> *Dear Aunt Jean,*
> *How are you? I'm fine. School was good today. Tommy is a brat.*
> *I'm going to play with some friends now. Hope to see you this summer.*
> *Love,*
> *Hillary*

The chore accomplished and her mother appeased, Hillary forgot about the letter until the day Jean's reply arrived in the mail. It was Hillary's first letter from a grown-up that was not related to a birthday or holiday. Jean was delighted and surprised at Hillary's letter, and she asked about school, friends, and activities. From this tentative beginning, a rich correspondence grew, and every week or two Hillary and Jean exchanged letters. It was no coincidence that Hillary's handwriting, spelling, grammar, and punctuation improved remarkably. The reports, stories, and poems Hillary attached to her letters received special care. Neither nagging nor encouragement was necessary for Hillary to write. She loved getting mail and knew that the best way to get mail was to send it.

THE POWER OF LISTENING

Jean and her sister, Hillary's mother, understood that children frequently do not express themselves or reveal details because they assume that adults do not really listen to them. They want to talk and share details, but adults are frequently unfocused and preoccupied, and the first distraction—the telephone, another child, or most likely, another adult—robs the child of her audience. At other times, the child attempts to explain something, but another impatient inquiry from the adult interrupts the child in midsentence. The revelations of the child therefore become more perfunctory until the conversation ends with single words. In contrast, when a child sends a letter and receives a response that indicates a careful reading along with questions soliciting more detail, the child has found a listener. This listener is an adult who takes the child seriously, reads every word without interruption, and sincerely wants to know more. In the words of a wise nine-year-old, "Nobody can interrupt me when they are reading my letter."

MOTIVATING CHILDREN TO WRITE LETTERS

Motivation is a hotly debated issue among educators and psychologists. Some experts hold that children need clear structure for behavioral expectations, including rewards and consequences. Others claim that incentives and sanctions work only in the short term and do not provide lasting self-motivation. They insist that long-term motivation must be internally generated and that children must pursue their own interests. As is frequently true in such matters, it is not an either/or proposition. Sometimes parents insist that children do things or avoid bad behavior whether or not the child is motivated to comply. Before they touch the hot stove, we grab their hands. Even when they would rather play with holiday toys, we insist that they write thank-you notes. Ultimately, however, we trust that their personal need for safety will create an enduring aversion to hot stoves and that their feelings of being grown-up and appreciated will lead them to initiate the writing of thank-you notes. Hillary was not initially motivated to write, and the result of her forced writing was a letter that was curt and bland. Along with the move from a maternal imperative to self-sustained writing was a move from a three-sentence letter to multiple pages of well-crafted prose.

MOTIVATIONAL KEYS: CHOICE, POWER, AND COMPETENCE

If every letter from Hillary to Aunt Jean had to be prompted by a command from her mother, then Hillary's writing would have improved very little. The motivational keys that accompanied her journey from a tentative writer to an exemplary correspondent are the same elements common to all motivation: choice, power, and competence.

There are many ways that parents can provide more choice for children to begin the first key to motivation. We can offer a choice of time. "You choose. You can write the letter now or at five o'clock." We can offer a choice of subject. "You can write about anything you want. The most important thing is that you are writing about things that are interesting for you." We can offer a choice of recipient. "You don't have to write to Aunt Jean. If you prefer, you can write to Uncle Augustus or, for that matter, you can write to the editor of the newspaper, the president, or the zookeeper."

"Power" may seem an odd term to associate with children who, we assume, are necessarily powerless in a world largely governed by adults. That is precisely why power is so important for children. It is a rare feeling to be in control of something, particularly to have the feeling that they are exercising power over adults. The more accurate term for this motivating sense of personal empowerment is efficacy. This term has nothing to do with efficiency or effectiveness, though it is sometimes misused in those contexts. Psychologists define efficacy as an individual's sense of exerting control over present and future events. A child with the quality of efficacy will think, If I study, I will do better on the test, rather than, It doesn't make any difference what I do. It's just luck anyway. The efficacious child will reason, If I'm nice to her, then she will probably be nice to me, rather than, People are so strange. You never know what they are going to do and there's nothing that I can do about it. When we are building the motivational component of writing, efficacy grows over time. Children are not initially aware of the influence they have until they start seeing a response to their writing. In order to reduce the risk of disappointment and diminished sense of efficacy, parents should encourage multiple correspondences in case a recipient fails to respond. If children begin the habit of writing a letter just once every two weeks to various personal and public contacts, they will develop a rich and varied collection of adults who responded in a tangible and meaningful way to their actions.

Competence is the third key to motivation, and it is one that parents and teachers sometimes forget or deliberately ignore. Perhaps the reason that competence as a motivational factor is neglected by adults is that we too seldom take the risk to be a novice ourselves. We prefer to do what we are most comfortable doing. We find incompetence painful, awkward, and embarrassing. So do our kids. If we want them to become motivated writers, they must become competent writers. Therefore, we do precisely the wrong thing when we assume that children must always be in their "comfort zone" and fear that challenging them to revise and improve their work might be discouraging and harmful. The faster we build competence through our love, encouragement, coaching, and clear feedback, the more quickly this essential motivational key will replace the need for parental mandates.

LETTER IDEAS

Although relatives are usually a reliable source for responding to children's letters, here are some other ideas to generate both personal interest from your child and potential responses to their letters:

Previous Teachers

One of the best moments in a teacher's life is being thanked by former students. Sometimes years, even decades, pass before a student thanks a teacher for the enormous impact he or she had. Your child probably has had at least one special teacher. A letter containing not only sincere expressions of appreciation but also memories of fun times, new learning, and interesting activities will be heartwarming for both writer and reader.

Authors of Children's Books

Children often know the title of their favorite book, but they have not thought much about the author. My students have written to authors and received pictures, notes, and announcements of other books by the same author. Try these addresses for favorite authors:

J. K. Rowling (the *Harry Potter* series), Ann M. Martin (*The Baby-Sitters Club* series), K. A. Applegate (*Animorphs, Everworld*), R. L. Stine (the *Goosebumps* series):

Author's Name
c/o Scholastic, Inc.
557 Broadway
New York, NY 10012

• • •

Judy Blume (*Tales of a Fourth Grade Nothing*), Christopher Awdry (the more recent *Thomas the Tank Engine* series), Marc Brown (the *Arthur* series), Stan and Jan Berenstain (the *Berenstain Bears* series):

Author's Name
c/o Random House Children's Publishing
1540 Broadway
New York, NY 10036

• • •

Maurice Sendak (*Where the Wild Things Are*), Beverly Cleary (*Ramona*):
Author's Name

c/o HarperCollins Children's Books
1350 Avenue of the Americas
New York, NY 10019

• • •

Ian Falconer (the *Olivia* series), Judith Viorst (*Alexander and the Terrible, Horrible, No Good, Very Bad Day*):

Author's Name
c/o Simon & Schuster Children's Books
1230 Avenue of the Americas
New York, NY 10020

• • •

Madeleine L'Engle (*A Wrinkle in Time*):

Farrar, Straus, and Giroux
19 Union Square West
New York, NY 10003

• • •

❄The Name of Your School

This is problematic if your child attends George Washington Elementary School, but many elementary schools are named for prominent local or state people who may be unfamiliar to your child. Finding that person or their descendants and asking about them is a fascinating project that may lead to some interesting correspondence. In my own seventh-grade investigation of the man for whom my junior high school was named, I found his obituary column in the library microfilm and then wrote to his children. After a few false starts and wrong addresses, I received a gracious and detailed letter from the granddaughter of William Jardine, who was thrilled that a student took an interest in a man whose contributions to education had been forgotten by many. I confess that, with typical seventh-grade self-aggrandizement, I relished the thought that I knew more than the principal about the man for whom our school had been named.

Animal Advocates

Children are often passionate friends and protectors of animals. Several organizations that cater to this interest, including the National Wildlife Federation, the World Wildlife Fund, and National Geographic, publish letters from children in their newsletters and magazines for students. Their addresses are:

Ranger Rick magazine
National Wildlife Federation
11100 Wildlife Center Drive
Reston, VA 20190-5362

National Geographic World
National Geographic
P.O. Box 98199
Washington, D.C. 20090-8199

World Wildlife Fund
1250 24th Street NW
Washington, D.C. 20037

Children's Publications

There are a number of regional and national children's publications that welcome articles, drawings, and letters from children. National magazines with excellent reputations are *Stone Soup, Cricket, Highlights for Children,* and *U*S* Kids.* Many newspapers include kids' pages that are frequently written and edited by students and that print letters from readers. Addresses for the aforementioned publications:

Stone Soup
Children's Art Foundation
P.O. Box 83
Santa Cruz, CA 95063

Cricket
Cobblestone Publications
30 Grove Street, Suite C
Peterborough, NH 03458

Highlights for Children
P.O. Box 18275
Columbus, OH 43218

U*S* Kids
Benjamin Franklin Literary and Medical
Society
1100 Waterway Boulevard
Indianapolis, IN 46206

Unsung Heroes

Since September 11, 2001, students have sent millions of letters to firefighters, police offi-cers, medical workers, and other public servants who perform difficult, dangerous, and es-sential work. Help your child think of public servants who deserve recognition and appre-ciation. Some candidates might be in the school, including the secretary, maintenance workers, traffic safety patrols, and cafeteria staff. Other unsung heroes could include health care workers, particularly if you have a relative who receives extended nursing care or who has recently been in a hospital or other treatment center.

Your family could cover a wall with prospective recipients of your child's letters, and the longer the list, the more choices your child will have. As Hillary discovered, the re-wards of letter writing are not immediately obvious, and before it is a pleasure it may be a bothersome chore. The creation of letters provides, better than almost any other form of writing, a personal and individual audience for the ideas and words of your child. Both you and your children will find it worth the trouble.

14 Writing Descriptions

"my dog is named Frankie. He is Brown. He likes me the best. The end."

THIS IS THE sort of descriptive essay that leads teachers to despair and parents to offer a weak smile. Unfortunately, our eyes are immediately drawn to the errors in capitalization and spelling rather than to the heart of descriptive writing: the language that transforms words into pictures and actions into theater. The next draft of this essay will, we hope, include the corrections in mechanics. But it is equally important that we listen for changes in language.

ENCOURAGING RICH DESCRIPTION

The easiest way to encourage better description from student writers is to ask questions. Although it is tempting to offer direction and instruction, only questions elicit details. Our questions should focus both on the obvious elements of description—the details of appearance and action—and on the less apparent details of emotion, feelings, thoughts, and impressions. In order for questions to be effective, we should offer them one at a time and pause longer than usual for an answer. If we turn questions into interrogations, the child can become defensive. If, on the other hand, our questions stem from a genuine desire to know more, to learn something from the child, then we have a young person who experiences the unusual opportunity to teach an adult something. We also have an adult who experiences the unusual requirement to sit quietly and listen to a young teacher. Here are some questions that you can ask your child to elicit rich descriptions:

"Tell me more . . ."

"I loved what you wrote about Frankie. He sounds like a great dog. Would you tell me some more about him? You said that Frankie was brown. I wonder if you could draw a picture with words. Is he light or dark brown, or is he different colors in different places?" This is the beginning of a careful request for details. It is essential that we are clear about our motivations. It is not merely that we want more description, as if length were a substitute for detail. Rather, we really find Frankie interesting and know that our young writer has a great deal more to say, if only we can provide the interest and encouragement. Each question should be asked separately, not as part of a rapid-fire interrogation. Over the course of time, we can learn more not only about the color of Frankie's coat, but whether his hair is straight or curly, what color his eyes are, if he has bushy eyebrows, and for that matter, whether Frankie is really a "he" as we have presumed.

"What does he do?"

Questions about action open the door for description that extends beyond appearance. In response to these questions, we learn not only about size, shape, and color, but also about speed, direction, and many other characteristics of action. Each of these characteristics changes with context. "What does Frankie do when he first sees you come home?" we might ask. "How is that different from what Frankie does when you leave for school in the morning?" To further encourage the writer's description, we can ask, "When you think about Frankie, does it make you think of other things?" Without using the words *simile* or *metaphor,* parents can introduce the concept that effective description frequently compares the physical characteristics and actions of one thing to something that is more familiar. While the reader does not know anything about Frankie, the reader can understand the expression that, "When I was little, Frankie was bigger than I was, and it was a little scary. Each time he came up to me it was like being chased by a grizzly bear in the forest." While we haven't seen Frankie's irregular hair, we understand the imagery of the student who writes, "His fur is the craziest thing I've ever seen, sticking up in every different direction. He looks like my teenage brother when he has put gel in his hair and is going to a concert, except that Frankie doesn't do it on purpose." As we solicit more details about Frankie, we learn about every detail. The description of appearance created a picture, and with the vivid characteristics of action, we have a home movie. We are starting to see Frankie in our minds.

⚛ "How did you feel about it?"

Describing emotions is one of the most difficult parts of writing, regardless of the author's age. Whereas the adolescent and adult writer can go on for pages about the emotional reaction to events real or imagined, the young writer can be reduced to monosyllabic descriptions such as "mad," "sad," "glad," and "scared." In encouraging our children to write about emotions, we are laying the groundwork for candor and openness now and in future years. When they write about fear, for example, children think through the physical sensations of trembling hands, gasping for breath, and weak knees. When they write about sadness, they consider not only their tears, but how one's face can ache from crying, the damp surface of the pillowcase wet with fresh tears, and the contradictory feelings of resisting the embrace of a parent or sibling at the very time when they most need a hug.

The honest discussion of emotion may seem difficult, even painful. Parents must therefore consider what happens when children do not write about their emotions. Does the absence of writing eliminate the events and associated feelings of joy, anger, sadness, and fear? Although parents frequently say ridiculous things such as "Don't be sad" or "You shouldn't be angry," we ultimately learn that we cannot govern emotions, but can only listen and acknowledge them.

⚛ "How did you think about it?"

Descriptions of thought processes differ from written analyses of emotions. Whereas the challenge in writing about emotions is the creation of a description that is clear and complete, the analysis of thought patterns includes another difficult process—the search for errors. The analysis of thought processes may sound like a sophisticated requirement, but it is not beyond the ability of children in the early years of elementary school. For example, children can understand the difference between fiction and truth; that is, between stories that are imaginary and those that are real. At a more challenging level, children can understand the difference between claims that are assertions and statements that are supported by evidence. Teachers routinely engage second and third graders in critical thinking exercises in which students analyze the claims of advertisers and subject those claims to rigorous scrutiny. In my visits to schools around the nation, some of the most compelling evidence of critical thinking by students can be found in posters that display advertisements accompanied by "fact" and "fiction" columns. In the course of these assignments, students notice not only the obvious claims made explicitly in advertisements, but also the more subtle, implicit claims. They challenge the assertions implied by some advertising models, for example, that smoking is associated with the beautiful, tough, and cool.

In addition to distinguishing between assertion and evidence, children can identify other logical errors such as overgeneralization. Even when there is evidence present—the hamster is indeed brown—we cannot use that evidence to claim that all hamsters are brown. When children are writing about their own thought processes, it is a very useful exercise for them to confront and acknowledge potential analytical errors.

"Because I live with an older brother who is nice to me, I thought that all teenagers were nice. Last Saturday I learned that is not true." And thus begins a story about a scary incident of bullying in the park.

"She looks beautiful and cool," the essay begins, "and her clothes are amazing. But she's a smoker, and the advertisement might make you think that smoking will allow you to be beautiful and cool and wear nice clothes." The student has a strong beginning to an analysis of logical errors on which advertisers depend.

After the creation of a personal narrative and fanciful stories, the most common type of writing is description. Unfortunately, most descriptive writing stops with the superficialities of color and size. When we ask probing questions, our children will discover that they have more to say. When we then extend the description with our inquiries about action, emotions, and thought processes, the four-sentence description will become a piece of writing that is rich and captivating. As we become better listeners and questioners, our children become more careful observers and more engaging writers.

12 The Analytical Essay

AT FIRST blush, the very term "analytical essay" can seem intimidating to and even inappropriate for children in the early years of elementary school. In this chapter, we will demystify analytical writing, provide examples of how children can enjoy the creation of detailed, effective analyses and explain why this skill is essential.

The vast majority of writing in elementary school consists of fictional stories and personal narratives. Middle-school teachers tell me that most students are able to create characters, devise an interesting plot, and relate the events of their personal experience with little difficulty. But when the teacher asks students to "compare and contrast" characters from different novels or "analyze the causes" of an event in a history class or "analyze the components" of a substance in science class, the quality of student writing breaks down. The rich vocabulary and elegant transitions that were fixtures of the personal narrative and creative short fiction disappear, replaced with fragmentary lists and fractured ideas. If we want our children to enter middle school with success and confidence, then they must master the art of analytical writing long before they leave elementary school.

There is also the practical matter of tests in elementary school. A growing number of state tests require fourth- and fifth-grade students to write persuasive, descriptive, and analytical essays. Parents are bewildered when their bright child who brings home A's in writing receives an unsatisfactory rating on a state writing test. Often those A's were awarded for the demonstration of skills, such as excellent penmanship and creativity, that state tests do not measure. If children will be tested on their analytical writing skills, it is only fair to give them many opportunities over several years to perfect those skills.

Some parents and teachers have been led to believe that it is developmentally inappropriate to require elementary school children to engage in analytical writing. Although there are a variety of opinions among educators and parents about what children can and should do, this is an area where your common sense should take precedence over opinions. Consider the natural curiosity of children. One of the questions asked most frequently by toddlers is, "Why?" and their persistence in asking that question suggests that, with neither state tests nor teachers to guide them, children want to know about the world around them. In fact, a genuine response to their developmental readiness might suggest that the consideration of analytical writing and discussions in fourth or fifth grades is several years too late.

WHAT IS ANALYSIS?

There are three types of analytical writing: parts of a whole, cause and effect, and similarities and differences. All three are within the grasp of elementary school students provided they receive the training and the practice.

Parts of a Whole

While a substance such as dirt may appear to be a single material, an investigation of dirt under a microscope reveals many different components, each with different properties, colors, and shapes. Long before kindergarten, most children have taken apart a toy or built an elaborate tower from blocks, only to knock it down and start over again. A desire to understand the relationship of the parts to a whole seems to be a natural inquiry of children. The opportunities for exploring the relationship between the parts of a whole can be found in every class. In social studies classes, children learn that states are part of a country, that counties are part of a state, and that cities are part of a county. In music students learn that stanzas are part of a song. In art class students learn that colors are part of a spectrum, and that many colors are combinations of other colors.

Cause and Effect

"Why is the sky blue?" our children ask. The analysis of cause and effect is also an understanding that children seek early in life. "Why do birds sing?" they want to know. "What makes the car go fast?" Many ancient myths stem from the innately human desire to understand the world, and thus elaborate stories surrounding the origins of flowers and the movements of the sun, moon, and stars were created as part of oral tradition, then pictorial representation, and ultimately as part of our literary history. Other myths sought to explain not only the physical world, but the emotional characteristics of humans, providing historical backgrounds for jealousy, generosity, bravery, and covetousness. In more recent times, children's books, such as Kipling's *Just So Stories* offered fanciful explanations of "How the elephant got its trunk," and other curiosities that amused children and their parents. These myths and stories reveal our primal desire to understand cause and effect in the world around us. When we challenge children to write about causes and effects—whether they are inventing their own myths or engaging in a factual explanation of evaporation, condensation, and rain—they satisfy one of the most basic human desires, to explore and to understand. This breakthrough to understanding about the world around us is, for children and adults, as interesting as an engaging personal narrative or a fanciful story.

Elementary social studies classes offer countless opportunities to explore cause and effect. Professor Richard Elmore, of the Harvard University Graduate School of Education, recently shared a story about his visit to a fourth-grade classroom. "What are you learning about?" Professor Elmore inquired of one student.

"The Civil War," the student began. "You see, you have to understand the economic causes as well as the political causes. Cotton was a major crop in the South in the 1800s . . ."

As Dick finished the story, he mused that most people would not expect to see an inner-city fourth grader lecturing a Harvard professor on the causes of the Civil War.

"Compare and Contrast"

If we were to limit analytical writing to the parts of a whole and cause and effect, most parents and teachers would have little difficulty accepting the relevance, importance, and fun of such writing in the elementary grades. But the words "compare and contrast" conjure up images of a blue essay booklet, a large auditorium, a humorless professor, and a clock ticking away the minutes that expired long before we were able to explicate the similarities and differences between the French and American revolutions, the Reformation and Counterreformation, and the African and Asian Anti-Colonialist movements. How in the world can this kind of writing be appropriate for elementary schoolchildren? Once again, I turn to my student writers for the answer.

When we challenge students to "compare and contrast," we are really asking about similarities and differences. One of the best ways to begin this investigation is with a Compare and Contrast Chart or "T-Chart" (Figure 12.1). The two things being compared are identified in the title for each column. Within each column, the student identifies the similarities and the differences.

Compare this:_____	To this: _____
How is it similar?	**How is it similar?**
How is it different?	**How is it different?**

Figure 12.1. Compare and Contrast Chart ("T-Chart")

Opportunities to explore similarities and differences are all around us. In the yard or a park, children can consider how trees are similar and different. A trip to the zoo offers endless opportunities for such comparisons. As children become keener observers of the natural world, they will relish challenges in finding differences among things that seem, on the surface, to be quite similar. Literature offers the opportunity for children to take a second look at characters, settings, and plots that they have read but not yet considered in great detail. We can consider different characters within a single book, exploring their personalities, attitudes, and use of language. At a more sophisticated level, children can explore the similarities and differences between characters in different books, making connections that are not immediately obvious even to adult readers. By first inviting children to explore the similarities between familiar characters—the spider and the pig in *Charlotte's Web,* for example—we can begin a more complex journey into a comparison of characters in different novels. For example, we can compare the gallantry and gentleness of Charlotte to that of the Abbot of Redwall (from the splendid series by that name created by Brian Jacques), and to mythological characters who sacrificed their lives and are memorialized as constellations. Such adventures in analytical writing lay the groundwork for deep thinking, reading, and reflection in the years ahead.

ANALYTICAL WRITING: A CASE STUDY

Some parents are concerned about the impact of popular movies on the literary appetites of children. "If kids can watch the movie," parents reason, "why would they bother reading the book?" One eight-year-old writer will help us answer that question, and his findings might help your own children address the question as well. Why, after all, should they bother reading the book? Although some parents have expressed concern about the literary merit of the Harry Potter series by the British author J. K. Rowling, most of us are thrilled to see children so engaged in reading. Since the publication of the first volume in the series, millions of children have been hefting the five-hundred-page books around to school, reading in preference to watching television at home, and holding a flashlight under the covers to read after parents have tucked them into bed. I was concerned that the movie *Harry Potter and the Sorcerer's Stone* would dampen enthusiasm for reading the book. My student writers have, once again, taught me a lesson. Figure 12.2 contains the T-Chart that was created in response to the challenge, "Compare the Harry Potter movie to the book. How are they similar? How are they different?"

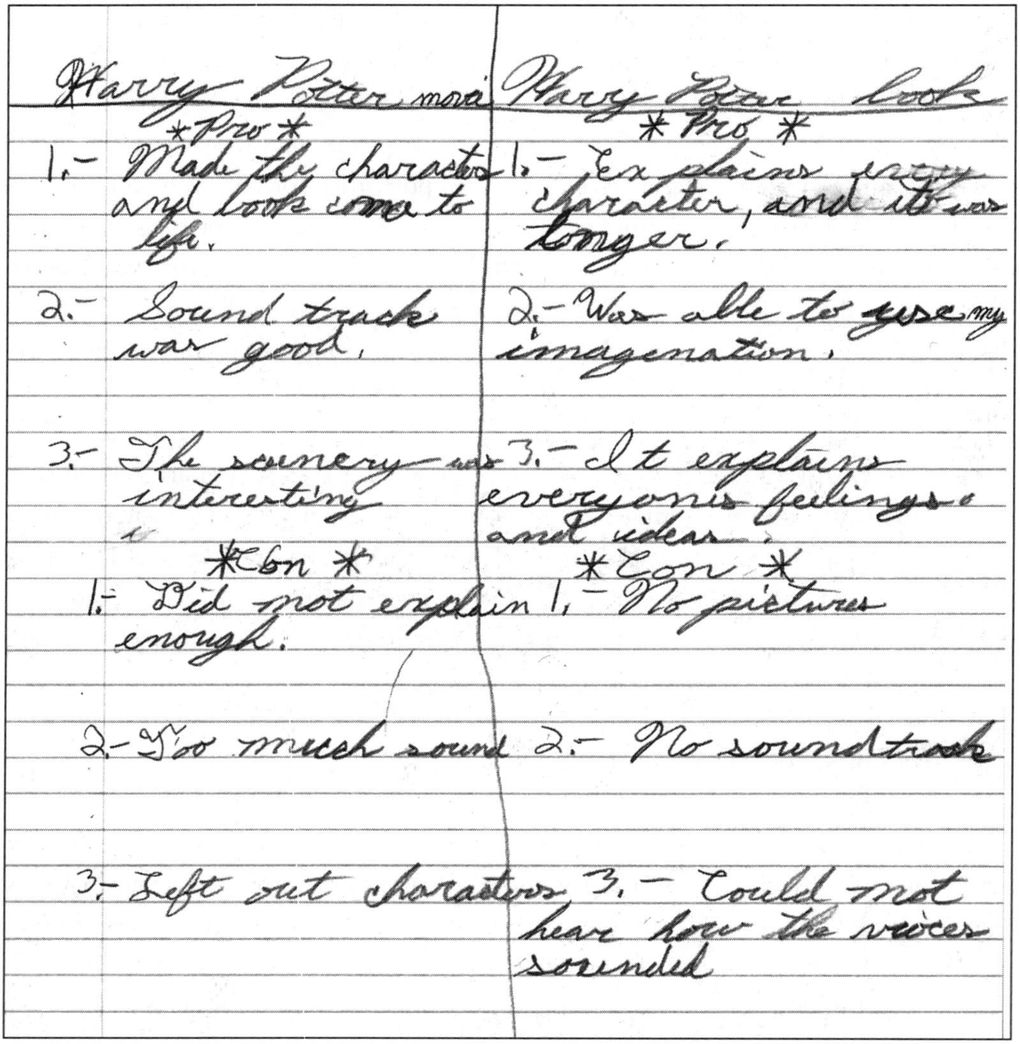

Harry Potter movie | Harry Potter book
Pro | *Pro*

1.- Made the characters and book come to life. | 1.- Explains every character, and it was longer.

2.- Sound track was good. | 2.- Was able to use my imagination.

3.- The scenery was interesting | 3.- It explains everyone's feelings and ideas.

Con | *Con*

1.- Did not explain enough. | 1.- No pictures

2.- Too much sound | 2.- No sound track

3.- Left out characters | 3.- Could not hear how the voices sounded

Figure 12.2. A T-Chart on Harry Potter

During the creation of this Compare and Contrast Chart, the writer exchanged ideas with friends, made a few corrections, and reflected on the enormous quantity of detail in the characters, plots, and settings of the movie and book. This detailed analysis also gave the student a better appreciation of how the characters have evolved from one Harry Potter book to the next. In the following essay (Figure 12.3), he proceeds from factual analysis to interpretation and finally an evaluation. While by no means perfect in every convention of English expression, the essay nevertheless represents what an eight-year-old can do when provided an engaging topic and a methodical structure for organizing his ideas.

Harry Potter: The Book vs. The Movie.

This paper is about the comparison between the book and the Movie of Harry Potter. The things that I liked and disliked About both will be stated in this essay.

After reading the book, The Sorcerers stone; I decided to see the Movie because I wanted to see the book come to life with action-packed Adventures. I wanted to see how each character acted and what their voices sounded like.

In the book I imagined what they talked like and looked because there are no pictures. In the movie I was able to see and hear what they were like.

The scenery in the book, was better because I could use my imagination, However the movie brought it to life.

In the book, using my imagination, I knew what they were thinking. However in the movie I was able to hear what they were thinking.

I liked the book better because they explained everything and had more characters. I enjoyed the movie because it followed the book.

Figure 12.3. An Essay on Harry Potter

I visited a third-grade class not long ago and asked to review the writing folders. The teacher was delighted to share twenty-three folders, each of which contained many writing samples for each child. Although I was pleased to see that the teacher took evident pride in student writing, I was dismayed by the repetitive nature of the content. I started making marks on a pad for each type of writing that I encountered, and found that there was a 90:1 ratio of fiction to nonfiction writing. These children will leave the third grade thinking that they are great writers and will face bewilderment and anxiety when their fourth-grade teacher asks for analytical writing. Of course, stories are important. Certainly personal narratives have value. But parents and teachers must encourage elementary students at *every* level to use the analytical skills they began to develop the first time they asked "Why?" as a two-year-old.

ANALYTICAL ESSAY PROMPTS

If your child is not getting enough practice writing analytical essays in school, or if you simply want to provide your child with a stimulating and rewarding exercise, ask your child to choose one of the following writing prompts for an essay, or invite him to think of one on his own.

Parts of a Whole

• Car engines
• My favorite toy
• My family
• Flowers
• Solar system
• My favorite food
• A quilt
• Skyscrapers
• My favorite song
• A sports team

Cause and Effect

- Sunrises
- Seasons
- The common cold
- Why I get mad/happy/sad
- Why the Civil War started
- Why some Native Americans live on reservations
- Why Social Security exists
- Leap year
- What causes light bulbs to shine
- What makes me do my very best work

Compare/Contrast

- Harry Potter's two best friends (Hermione and Ron)
- Batman and Superman
- My two favorite movies
- My two favorite books
- My two favorite sports teams
- Modern armies and Sauron's forces (Tolkien's *The Lord of the Rings*)
- Barbie and G.I. Joe
- My life and my parents' lives when they were my age
- My best friend and me
- My house and my grandparents' house

13 The Persuasive Essay

PERSUASIVE WRITING is an increasingly common requirement for students in the upper elementary grades and throughout middle and high school. More important, persuasive writing is a lifelong skill that students will use in their communications with colleagues, employers, public officials, and, one day, their own children. The formal term "essay" should not prevent the strong association between persuasion and passion. We need the skill of persuasion to effect change.

We also need persuasive writing skills to protect and maintain those things we value, from a species threatened with extinction to a family tradition that is in danger of neglect. We persuade, in other words, to influence the actions and beliefs of others.

Nine-year-old Martha has not taken much time to dissect the need for persuasive writing. She likes reading and writing well enough, but school is school and, compared to the excitement of her friends, animals, and activities, school activities are not the sort of things she associates with passion and deep belief. Nevertheless, Martha already has experienced the power of writing. She recalls the thrill when her soccer coach changed position assignments based on a thoughtful letter from Martha that included appeals to both effective strategy and fundamental fairness. Words on paper, she found, can influence people, including adults. Although she did not regard her letter as a persuasive essay, clearly she produced something with greater impact than the typical stories, essays, and notes that she had produced in her brief career as a writer.

FROM "I FEEL" TO EVIDENCE AND ACTION

In the previous chapter, we recalled the penchant for toddlers to ask the question, "Why?" When very young children respond to that question, they frequently offer the one-word response, perhaps emulating their elders, "Because." When prompted for some elaboration, the young child offers little more than, "Because I want to!" or "Because I said so!" They regard the requirement for explanation with exasperation, an intrusion into the straight line that should, in a just world, connect their desires to the fulfillment of their wishes. In the early years of elementary school, most students' reasoning has not advanced a great deal. The telltale phrase "I feel" dominates early attempts at persuasion by most writers, including those well past elementary school. Even in those rare cases where students can find evidence to support their indignation (persuasive essays with student-selected topics are almost always about something that makes the student mad), young writers find it easier to articulate the reasons they are upset than to use the available evidence to suggest an appropriate course of action. They can, in other words, express concern about the rain forest, but fail to explain what should be done about it.

PEAS AND PERSUASIVE WRITING

In helping our children to compose persuasive essays, we can ask them to bear in mind the acronym PEAS. If they have a particular dislike for peas, as I do, then all the better. We are, after all, writing about things that make us mad. PEAS stands for Problem, Evidence, Arguments, and Solution. In the topic sentence and first paragraph, students should briefly state the problem. The introductory paragraph can also foreshadow the evidence, arguments, and solutions to come. In the next paragraph, the writer presents the evidence. By leading with facts, the writer makes clear that this essay is not based on personal prejudice and unsubstantiated views. Facts are friends, and good persuasive writers build a strong foundation for their arguments by presenting the factual arguments in clear and convincing detail.

The third paragraph in the PEAS formula contains the arguments. Based on what we know from the facts presented in the second paragraph, what inferences can we draw? There is a strong similarity between this format and the scientific method in which students writing a lab report record their results first and then follow with their interpretation of those results. This stands in stark contrast to the typical persuasive essay of students and adults in which the writer leads with arguments and then appears to search frantically, often vainly, for evidence to support them. The final paragraph articulates the solution. Considering the problem, evidence, and arguments, what should the reader do? The best persuasive essays contain a direct request for action. "Go out and buy this book!" "Don't you dare see that movie!" "Don't give this toy to a child under five!" "Vote for the school bond issue!" "Don't send your kid to summer camp!" "Give money to New York libraries!" "Thank your kid's teacher!" Calls for action by children seem imperious and demanding when they are blurted out as a conversation starter. When the same demands come at the end of an essay that includes a succinct statement of the problem, powerful evidence, and thoughtful arguments, then readers should take heed. We are dealing with a persuasive writer here.

PERSUASIVE WRITING: A CASE STUDY

Figure 13.1 represents Rachel's first draft of a persuasive essay. Although this fifth grader clearly feels strongly about the subject at hand, her reasoning is unclear and the evidentiary links to the writing seem tenuous. Figure 13.2 is Rachel's draft using the PEAS formula of Problem, Evidence, Argument, and Solution. There is an interesting parallel between these two essays and the illustrations in chapter 7 on the power of pre-writing and organization. When James's initial single paragraph of observations about sound grew to several detailed and well-organized paragraphs, he had not engaged in additional study or reading. He simply organized what he already knew in a more thoughtful manner. Similarly, Rachel's fine essay in Figure 13.2 is not the result of additional coaching, study, or research. By using the small suggestion of an organizational framework, we were able to help Rachel show the reader much more of what she already knew.

PASSION + EVIDENCE = POWER

The emphasis we place on evidence, argumentation, and logic in the creation of a persuasive essay must not obscure what we know to be an essential element of great writing— the writer's passion. The best efforts of our children will stem not from our direction, but from their heartfelt involvement in a subject. In the practical world of educational assessment, children will sometimes be required to respond to an essay question or "prompt" that demands a narrowly directed response. Even under these circumstances, however, children should stop, think, and consider the aspects of that question that are most provocative. In addition to asking, "What does this mean?" they should ponder, "What does this mean to me?" Only when writers make such a personal connection can they bring the creative energy of personal narratives and fantastic fiction to the persuasive essay.

WEAR YOUR SEAT BELT

As you know, a child in our town was killed in a car wreck last week. He wasn't wearing a seat belt. Everybody knows that seat belts save lives, and I don't know why that kid's parent didn't make him wear his seat belt. Maybe he didn't want to. But people who ride in cars shouldn't have a choice. The driver needs to make everybody wear a seat belt.

The kid's name was Anthony. My mom said that she knew Anthony's mom, and that it was just a horrible accident. She said that they were on their way to soccer practice and that they were running late. She just didn't check to see that he was wearing his seat belt, or maybe Anthony was trying to tie his shoes and took his seat belt off. It was only for a few minutes. Then a truck came through the intersection and hit the car. Anthony died right away.

The problem is that lots of kids are not wearing seat belts. Even in our family, there are times when we forget, or we mess around in the car, or even my parents don't wear their seat belts. I've heard some kids say that if you are sitting in the backseat, you don't have to wear a seat belt, but that's wrong. In class we read a *New York Times* article that said that when people in the backseat do not wear seat belts, they can act as "human missiles" and hurt or kill people in the front seat during a car wreck. The article said that if everyone in the backseat wore seat belts, it would have saved more than 700 deaths and more than 1,500 injuries to people in the front seats of cars. If you don't wear a seat belt, the risk of getting killed is 17 times greater than if you do wear one. Princess Di wasn't wearing a seat belt, and she died. But only about 69 percent of people wear seat belts most of the time. If you're smart, you will wear your seat belt. If our city is smart, it will pass a law making everybody wear seat belts. Where there are fines if you don't wear a seat belt, the percentage of people who use seat belts goes up over 10 percent and more lives would be saved.

Figure 13.1. Rachel's First Draft of a Persuasive Essay

Rachel has done her research and offers both examples and statistics to bolster her arguments. In her writing conference, another student said, "I really liked your facts and numbers. In fact, I wish that you'd put them earlier in the essay so they would grab our attention. Try the PEAS outline—you know, Problem, Evidence, Arguments, and Solution." Another asked, "What about Anthony?" "It's terrible!" Rachel almost shouted. "He was just a kid and he wasn't wearing a seat belt!" Her friend offered, "You seem a lot more upset about it now than you did in the essay." Rachel thought about these comments and then completed her second draft.

ANTHONY'S LAW

I didn't know either Anthony, a kid on a local soccer team, or Diana, the beautiful Princess of Wales. But I know that they would both be alive today if they had worn their seat belts. A lot of people were sad about Princess Di, but we should be mad about Anthony. He didn't have to die. Seat belts save lives. Every kid knows that. But almost one-third of people don't wear seat belts. If you are one of those people, or if you let kids sitting in the same car with you get by without wearing their seat belts, then think about these facts.

Only 69 percent of people wear seat belts most of the time. People who are not wearing seat belts are 17 times more likely to die in a car accident than people who do wear seat belts. If you think that people in the backseat don't need to wear seat belts, think again. According to an article in the *New York Times,* passengers who don't wear seat belts are not only more likely to die in a car accident, but if they are sitting in the backseat, they are likely to kill somebody in the front when they become a "human missile" and, without a seat belt holding them down, hit someone in the front seat. If only people in the backseats of cars would wear seat belts all the time, it could save over 700 deaths and 1,500 injuries each year.

What does this information tell us? It tells us that even when the right thing to do is obvious, a lot of people don't do it. Even when people love their kids, they don't make them wear seat belts. Even when people are careful about their personal safety when they are cooking dinner or mowing the lawn, they don't do one of the easiest things in the world to save their lives. Even when the facts are clear and easy to understand, people don't use those facts to save their own lives and the lives of their children.

The solution is a law requiring seat belt use for every passenger, with stiff penalties for people who break that law. In a few cities where this kind of law has been passed, seat belt use goes up over 10 percent. Write to the mayor and town council today. Tell them that we need a law requiring seat belts passed today. Maybe they can call it "Anthony's Law." How many more people, including kids like Anthony, have to die before we listen to the facts and make seat belt use the law?

Figure 13.2. Rachel's Persuasive Essay Using PEAS Structure

14 The Research Paper

"**YOU'VE GOT TO BE** kidding!" exclaimed Richard. "I didn't have to do a research paper until I was a senior in high school, and now they want my fourth grader to do this? This is insane!" Like Richard, many parents are surprised at the requirements for research papers in elementary school. They recall their first research paper as a rite of passage. Having safely traversed the tortuous path through adolescence, only one academic obstacle remained—the senior paper. For the first time, the student confronted footnotes, citations, and a paper that extended ideas beyond two or three pages. The completion of that research paper often marked the first all-nighter, or at least the first all-nighter devoted to academic work. And now they want preadolescent children to do what most parents only experienced as a wizened seventeen-year-old?

WHAT IS A RESEARCH PAPER AND WHY DO KIDS NEED TO WRITE IT?

We have already seen ample proof that elementary school students can use evidence to support their ideas. Students surprise us with their sophistication, as third grader James did with his analysis of sound and as fifth grader Sophie did with her persuasive writing. Although student mythology places the research paper on an elevated plane far above mortal writing, in fact research papers are just one more step on the continuum of writing. Fourth and fifth graders can isolate a research question, organize an outline, find primary and secondary sources, use evidence to support ideas, cite sources, and create bibliographies.

The research papers constructed in the vast majority of today's schools, elementary as well as secondary, are not the frantic jumble of last-minute tasks that parents may recall from their youth. Today's elementary school students have the opportunity to gain confidence and competence for their future challenges in secondary school and college. I have had students in graduate school who privately confessed that they had never, throughout secondary school and undergraduate school, written a research paper. Their graduate school experiences were, to say the least, miserable. Those few students who had created many research papers from their earliest school years through college were able to undertake the challenges of graduate school with confidence. The teachers who ask elementary students to write research papers are performing an exceptional service, provided that they help children approach the project in a carefully orchestrated, step-by-step fashion.

RESEARCH PAPER PROCEDURES

Completing a research paper is like assembling a puzzle. While the complexity of the puzzle grows as students get older, the essential steps to solving the puzzle remain the same. Similarly, the procedures for a good research paper are consistent from elementary through high school. The best teachers provide careful feedback after each step. Whether or not your child's teacher provides such intermediate feedback, you can dramatically reduce the stress and anxiety your child will feel about a research paper if you help break the project down into these ten steps:

1. Make a list of research questions.
2. Conduct a preliminary investigation.
3. Select a topic.
4. Draw up a first outline.
5. Make a set of bibliographic cards.
6. Make a set of research cards.
7. Construct a final outline based on the research cards.
8. Write a first draft based on the final outline.
9. Check the first draft for format and readability.
10. Write a second draft, incorporating corrections from Step 9.

STEP 1

Make a List of Research Questions

Research papers answer a question. They are not merely descriptions of a topic; that is, one does not do a research paper "about dinosaurs." Rather, the researcher begins with a question and then assembles evidence that answers this question. For example, if students are interested in dinosaurs, they might ask:

Why did dinosaurs become extinct?
How do scientists make dinosaur models in the museum?
What did dinosaurs eat and how do we know it?

Sometimes teachers will give students a defined topic, but more frequently the field of inquiry will be very broad. It is therefore up to students to find an aspect of the subject that engages their interests and offers the opportunity for research. By phrasing the topic in the form of a question, students will find it much easier to direct their research. If their topic is "all about dinosaurs," they will at first be delighted at the abundant resources in the library and will cart home a stack of books as tall as they are. But that exuberance will quickly give way to frustration as the task of researching all that material becomes overwhelming. The use of a research question to guide the enterprise will save time and reduce anxiety.

STEP 2

Conduct a Preliminary Investigation

In many cases, students delay the start of their research until they are well into the process of writing a research paper. They may already be committed to a topic and perhaps have drafted an outline, only to discover that they cannot find the research they had counted on, or that the topic is excessively broad or narrow. A preliminary investigation should take less than an hour. Initially, students should share their research question with a school or community librarian. These professionals are invariably happy to be asked for help, and their knowledge of available resources and grade-appropriate reading material is extensive.

Guided by the librarian, the student should read a few pages of available material, including three or four pages in a book about the subject and three or four pages in a magazine or journal. At this point, the student can consider whether the research question is any fun. "Is this really as interesting as I thought it was going to be?" If not, it is very early in the process and it may be wise to select another topic and a different research question. The student can also consider whether the research question is too broad or too narrow. If the research available is exceptionally abundant and almost overwhelming, then a narrower question might be in order. Rather than investigate the diet of all dinosaurs, for example, it might be better to ask about the diet of the Tyrannosaurus rex. If the research available is scant, now is the time to find out. Research papers for fourth- and fifth-grade students typically require five to seven sources. If the first venture to the library does not yield at least that many sources, then it is time to consider a different topic.

Some readers may wonder why a trip to the old-fashioned library is even necessary. Why not just conduct an Internet search? My children have tried that, with unsatisfactory results. Conduct a search for "dinosaurs," for example, and you will find over 23,000 possible entries, many of which include factually inaccurate information. Moreover, the results of an Internet search are not necessarily grade-appropriate or related to your child's research question. While it is appropriate to use technology and learn how to conduct an Internet search, that is a task far better accomplished later in the research paper process than during the preliminary inquiry. Moreover, because students tend to use Internet resources indiscriminately and tend to quote from them to pad the length of their papers, a number of teachers require that at least half of the references used in the paper come from books, journals, magazines, interviews, or historical documents.

STEP 3

Select a Topic

Wait a minute. Didn't we already select the topic? Not really. In almost every case, the research question is not the final topic. It may be a good start, but most students begin with a question that is too broad or too narrow. Before a student becomes irrevocably committed to a topic, this step is the opportunity to stop and ask, "What did I learn from my preliminary investigation? Should I change my topic?" If the answer to the latter question is yes, then the student should choose another question from the list made in Step 1 and repeat

Steps 2 and 3. Remember that just because a topic seems too broad does not mean it should be abandoned altogether. Sometimes a bit of preliminary research can narrow the scope of questions that would make more appropriate research topics.

STEP 4

Draw Up a First Outline

For some students, the elementary school research project is their first introduction to outlining. For other students, outlining may be limited to the use of Roman numerals and the organization of items into main headings and subordinate headings. In the case of the research paper, the outline follows a reasonably consistent format. See Figures 14.1 and 14.2 for two examples of research paper outlines. The exact words that your child may use will not be the same as those contained in these examples, particularly for parts II, III, and IV of the outline. Rather, the student must know enough about the topic to understand what the "big ideas" are and the important information surrounding those big ideas. If the research paper is descriptive in nature, then the "big idea" approach of the first outline will work better; if the research paper is directed to a question, then the "possible answer" approach of the second outline will probably be easier to use.

It is very important to note that at this stage of research, the student probably will not have enough information to complete an outline this detailed. In fact, the student may have only the main headings, as expressed in Roman numerals, identified. That is the reason that this is only the first outline. Only after additional research and reading can the additional substructure of the outline be created.

I. Introduction

   A. Research question

   B. Reason the topic is interesting and important

   C. Very brief summary of the paper

II. Big Idea #1

   A. Identify the idea

   B. Explain the idea

   C. Relate the idea to your research question

III. Big Idea #2

   A. Identify the idea

   B. Explain the idea

   C. Relate the idea to your research question

IV. Big Idea #3

   A. Identify the idea

   B. Explain the idea

   C. Relate the idea to your research question

V. Conclusion

   A. Restate the research question

   B. Summarize the big ideas

   C. Express a conclusion that directly answers the research question

   D. Additional questions: What did you want to learn more about as a result of this research?

Figure 14.1. The "Big Idea" Outline for Research Papers

I. Introduction
  A. Research question
  B. Reason the topic is interesting and important
  C. Possible answers to the question

II. Possible Answer #1

  A. Identify the answer
  B. Explain the answer
  C. Evaluate the answer. Is it correct? Why?

III. Possible Answer #2

  A. Identify the answer
  B. Explain the answer
  C. Evaluate the answer. Is it correct? Why?

IV. Possible Answer #3

  A. Identify the answer
  B. Explain the answer
  C. Evaluate the answer. Is it correct? Why?

V. Conclusion

  A. Restate the research question
  B. Summarize the alternative answers
  C. Express a conclusion. Which answer is correct? Directly answer the research question.
  D. Identify additional questions. What did you want to learn more about as a result of this research?

Fisgure 14.2. "Alternative Answers" Outline for Research Papers

Make a Set of Bibliographic Cards

For most students, one of the most tedious parts of their first research paper is the format of the bibliography and the peculiar way in which research is identified. In the past, if a teacher or parent wanted to know how a child knew something, a sufficient response might have been, "I read it in a book," or, "I saw it in a magazine." In a research paper, however, students begin a habit that will endure throughout their academic career and, indeed, throughout their lifetime: giving credit to other people when using their ideas. It is very important that parents and teachers help children to understand that the use of bibliographic source information is not simply a format drill created by teachers to make students miserable. In fact, it is an ethical principle based on the need for fairness, something that every child understands. Your child might have felt the sting of seeing another student claim credit for an idea or an accomplishment. It hurt, and it was not fair. It even felt as if the other student was stealing something, and that is, indeed, the case. It is the same when student writers use the ideas and accomplishments of others when they write a research paper or an essay. We use bibliographic citations, not because of the style manual, but because we have an ethical obligation to honor the other writers whose research and writing helped us to understand the topic.

Students should create a separate card for each source. If there are three different articles that are used in the same issue of a magazine, that will require three different cards. The format of bibliographic cards will vary from one teacher to another. Typically, in elementary school, teachers are not using a very advanced style manual. Nevertheless, the thing to remember when getting information from a book, magazine, or other source is the maxim, "It is better to have information and not need it than to need information and not have it." Bibliographic cards for books should answer the following questions:

1. What is the title? What is the subtitle?
2. What is the name of the author (or authors, if there are more than one)?
3. What is the name of the editor?
4. What is the copyright date?
5. What is the name of the publisher?
6. In what city was it published?
7. How many pages is it?

For magazines, students should record answers to these questions on their bibliographic cards:

1. What is the full name of the author(s)?
2. What is the title of the article?
3. What is the full name of the magazine, newspaper, or journal?
4. What is the date of the magazine, newspaper, or journal?
5. What are the volume and issue numbers?
6. What are the page numbers on which the article appears?

For Internet citations (which may include excerpts from books, magazines, newspapers, or other sources), students must include not only all the information noted above, such as author, title, date, etc., but must also include the complete Internet address. Some of these addresses are long and confusing, but the reader of the research report must be able to trace any source used by the writer. That is the reason that full source citations are absolutely necessary. If the student is careful to follow the teacher's preferred bibliographic style in the creation of the cards, then it will be much easier to create the bibliography at the end of paper.

Walter, Martin S. "New Day Dawns in New York." *Monthly Magnet,* Vol. 32, no. 12, December 2001, pages 2–6.

Figure 14.3 Bibliographic Card: Magazine or Journal

Ellis, Dave. *Becoming a Master Student: Tools, techniques, hints, ideas, illustrations, examples, methods, procedures, processes, skills, resources, and suggestions for success.* Boston: Houghton Mifflin Company, 2001. 398 pages.

Figure 14.4 Bibliographic Card: Book

Haunshek, E. A. "Have We Learned Anything New? The RAND Study of NAEP Performance," *Education Matters More.* www.edmattersmore.org/2001sp/haunshek.html.

[Note: You must put the complete Internet address at the end of the title and journal information. The reason for this is that the reader must be able to find exactly the same information you used for your research paper.]

Figure 14.5 Bibliographic Card: Internet

Make a Set of Research Cards

Research cards should contain direct quotations from the sources used. Later in the process of writing the paper, students can paraphrase the text or extract a necessary statistic from the card. The research cards themselves, however, should have the exact quotation. The difference between a paraphrase and direct quotation is important for both stylistic and ethical reasons. If a writer quotes a source directly, using the exact words that appear in the text and on the research card, then quotation marks must appear around that material in the student's paper. If the writer uses different words to describe the same idea as the original document, then quotation marks are not required, but a footnote is necessary. For elementary school research papers, the true footnotes, with the bibliographic source appearing at the bottom of the page, are rarely used. Rather, most teachers require that students put the name of the source followed by the date in parenthesis after the paraphrase or quotation. For example, the original source might contain this information from a research card:

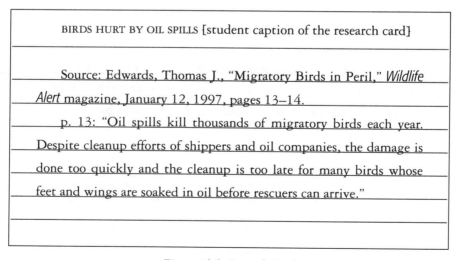

BIRDS HURT BY OIL SPILLS {student caption of the research card}

Source: Edwards, Thomas J., "Migratory Birds in Peril," *Wildlife Alert* magazine, January 12, 1997, pages 13–14.

p. 13: "Oil spills kill thousands of migratory birds each year. Despite cleanup efforts of shippers and oil companies, the damage is done too quickly and the cleanup is too late for many birds whose feet and wings are soaked in oil before rescuers can arrive."

Figure 14.6. Research Card

When this student uses this quotation in the paper as a paraphrase, it might appear as follows:

When oil spills happen, the companies responsible for the spill usually try to clean up the damage as quickly as possible. But for many birds, the cleanup is too late to save their lives (Edwards, 1997).

In most cases, there will be several research cards for each source. Each research card should contain only one important idea or piece of information. If an article or book has many different ideas, facts, or conclusions that the student finds interesting, each separate idea should have its own research card. The top of the card should have a few words that briefly describe the main idea of the card. The rest of the card should contain the source, the page number, and the exact quotation.

STEP 7

Construct a Final Outline Based on the Research Cards

With the research completed, the writer has a better idea of the details that link the research to the outline. One practice that I have found to be particularly effective is to lay out all the research cards on a table and see how they fit together. Place the preliminary outline on the same table. Just like the jigsaw puzzle, some pieces seem to fit while other pieces do not. All the cards about the first big idea or the first possible answer to the research question can be grouped together and placed toward the top of the table. All the cards about the second big idea or second possible answer to the research question belong in a separate pile, and so on. Now the writer is ready to use the research cards to create a much more detailed outline using the cards in each pile as specific ideas and evidence to support the main point of the outline. Depending on the amount of research your child has accumulated and the difficulty of the project, the final outline may be much more extensive than the preliminary outline. Whereas the preliminary outline used only Roman numerals and capital letters, the final outline might include numbers under some of the capital letters that will provide further elaboration.

It is important to note that, no matter how detailed with points and subpoints your child's outline is, it will be most helpful to use a complete sentence for every thought. Complete thoughts are preferable to items that contain one or two words. They will help focus the student's thought process and will aid immeasurably when it is time to begin writing. If every point in the final outline is made with a complete sentence, the student automatically has a topic sentence for almost every paragraph as he begins his first draft of the paper. Figure 14.7 provides an example of a more detailed final outline.

I. Introduction: We may know that dinosaurs all became extinct, but no one is sure why it happened.

  A. Why did the dinosaurs become extinct?

  B. It is important to think about why dinosaurs became extinct because it teaches us about our own world.

    1. Extinction might be necessary.

    2. Extinction might be avoidable.

    3. Dinosaur history can teach us valuable lessons.

  C. There are three main theories about how dinosaurs became extinct.

    1. There was a drastic change in the climate.

    2. An asteroid hit the earth.

    3. Food sources evolved too much.

II. Did a drastic change in the climate cause dinosaurs to become extinct?

  A. The climate suddenly became much colder.

  B. The climate change limited dinosaurs' food supply.

    1. Dinosaurs needed water.

    2. Freezing temperatures made water harder to get to.

    3. Freezing temperatures also caused plants and other food sources to die.

  C. Could the climate change theory be the right one?

    1. Some evidence supports it.

2. We still don't understand why the climate changed.

3. The climate changes do not explain all of the dinosaur deaths.

III. Did the dinosaurs die because of an asteroid?

  A. An asteroid may have hit the earth.

  B. A single asteroid could cause a worldwide impact.

    1. There would have been huge changes in climate.

    2. The asteroid would have polluted the atmosphere.

  C. Could the asteroid theory be the right one?

    1. There is evidence of asteroid craters.

    2. It would explain why large dinosaurs died in a short time period.

    3. It does not explain why some species survived.

IV. Did the evolution of food source cause the dinosaurs' extinction?

  A. If food sources evolved, it would affect dinosaurs' diet.

  B. Changes in some species cause changes to other species.

    1. All species evolve, change, and die.

    2. When a food source changes or dies, other species may loose their food source.

    3. Compared to other species, dinosaurs lived a long time and were very successful.

    4. Changes take place over millions of years, not in a short period of time.

  C. Could the food source theory be the right one?

    1. It is consistent with fossil evidence.

    2. It is also consistent with what we know of the dinosaurs' diet.

    3. Unfortunately, there is no clear evidence.

V. We must evaluate the possible theories of why the dinosaurs died.

A. Why did the dinosaurs become extinct?

B. The possible answers are a climate change, an asteroid, and a change in food supply.

C. All three answers may be correct.

D. There are other questions to research in the future.

1. Do species still become extinct?

2. What is happening to our food sources?

3. Is the climate still changing?

4. Do asteroids still hit the earth today?

Figure 14.7 Detailed Final Outline

STEP 8

Write a First Draft Based on the Final Outline

Using the final outline as a blueprint, the student is ready to create the first draft of the research paper. Teachers often provide a scoring guide, or rubric, for students to use to ensure that they are constructing the paper correctly. Parents should ask for a copy of this so that the student can conduct a thorough self-evaluation of the paper.

STEP 9

Check the First Draft for Format and Readability

It is often useful for students to have a friend read the first draft and answer the question gently but honestly, "Did I understand what the writer is saying?" For writers of any age, clarity is an extraordinary challenge. The information is quite clear, even obvious, to the writer who has read widely about the topic during the course of his research. A reader who lacks this extensive background, however, may be mystified. Perhaps the writer refers to things that are familiar to the writer but not to the reader. In a paper on dinosaurs, the writer may refer to the Paleolithic era, but the reader does not share the writer's knowledge about prehistoric periods. Perhaps the writer assumes that the reader understands the vocabulary related to the topic and refers to herbivores, but the reader does not know what that term means. A check for readability is one of the most helpful things one student can do for another. If parents are conducting the check for readability, it is essential that they adopt a perspective of deliberate naïveté, presuming that they are approaching the paper without a technical background in the subject. It is certainly no criticism and is, in fact, extremely helpful for a reader to say to a writer, "That's really interesting, but I don't understand it as well as you do. Please tell me more and help me understand it better."

The format check is also important. Teachers expect footnotes to be accurate, references to be complete, headings and subheadings to be in proper form, and the conventions of English grammar, spelling, and punctuation to be observed. It is almost impossible to check for format at the same time that you check for readability, so if you are reviewing your child's work, plan to read it twice. The first time, you will probably ask for more elaboration and explanation. The second time, you will help identify mechanical errors.

STEP 9

Write a Second Draft, Incorporating Corrections from Step 9

Depending on the feedback that the student receives in Step 9, there may be more than two drafts to the paper. My experience, however, is that if a student was careful and deliberate in the first eight steps, then two drafts are sufficient. If, on the other hand, students are too hasty in the construction of the outline or incomplete in the assembly of their research notes, and then rush to create the first draft, multiple drafts will be necessary. This is the case because the student is not only working on readability and format, but also filling in gaps in the outline, adding more research, and finding details from bibliographic citations. The work done in the beginning of the research paper process will save time and anxiety at the end of the process.

There is a delicate balance for parents in the review of the second draft. This is elementary school, not graduate school, and the work product of the child will fall short of the more sophisticated work that a parent might recall from high school– or college-level research papers. If children detect dissatisfaction at the difference between the quality of their parents' research papers (or at least the quality that parents remember) and the child's work product, then the stage is set for intellectual paralysis. Nothing will be good enough and the project will never be completed. As a wise teacher said to me when I was laboring excessively over a particular paper, "This is simply your current research project, not your last one. It is finished, let it go, and let's start thinking about your next project."

 CELEBRATE

Ask teenagers and adults what they remember about their first extensive project in elementary school. A few may recall the satisfaction of a job well done and some interesting things that they learned. Most responses, however, are likely to be chilling tales of late nights, confrontations with parents, and a sense that the work, however extraordinary, was not quite good enough. The time to influence your children's memories of schoolwork is now, and one of the best ways to do that is to celebrate significant achievements. Your celebration need not be elaborate or expensive. A family dinner with the child's favorite meal would be a great idea, along with the opportunity for your child to present the project, page by page and step by step, to the entire family. The sincere and undivided attention of others is one of the most encouraging and meaningful gifts a child can receive. In future years, your children are less likely to remember tangible rewards than those exquisite moments when they knew that their parents were proud of them.

RESEARCH PAPER STARTER QUESTIONS

Literature

- How was Mark Twain's *The Adventures of Huckleberry Finn* autobiographical?
- Were the working conditions for children portrayed in Dickens's novels historically accurate?
- What were the historical circumstances in which Louisa May Alcott wrote *Little Women*?
- Why do some people want to see certain books banned? (The child can choose a specific banned book and research the history of its censorship.)
- What were the historical circumstances in which Laura Ingalls Wilder wrote *Little House on the Prairie*?
- What was E. B. White's childhood like? (This can be applied to any author.)
- Where did Shakespeare get the plot for *Romeo and Juliet*?
- Where did Leonard Bernstein get the plot for *West Side Story*?

- Can any of *Aesop's Fables* be applied to the issues of today?
- How does Madeleine L'Engle's *A Wrinkle in Time* emphasize the importance of a close, loving family?

History

- What were the three main causes of the American Revolution?
- How was the town/city we live in first founded?
- How were women given the right to vote?
- What was the first organized government to give women the right to vote, and why?
- How did history influence the art of Norman Rockwell?
- How did history influence the music of the Baroque era?
- How has personal hygiene changed over the last three hundred years, and why?
- What were the three main causes of the Civil War?
- How does the Civil War compare to the Civil Rights movement?
- Who were the greatest leaders of the Civil Rights movement, and how did their beliefs compare to each other?
- How did jazz become an American art form?
- How were messages encoded in the songs of African-American slaves?
- How did the Industrial Revolution affect living conditions in Europe?

Science

- How do astronauts train to survive in space?
- How did George Washington Carver's innovations help our society?
- How did Thomas Edison's inventions influence our society?
- How does the Black Plague of medieval times compare with modern epidemics?
- What is the history of space travel?
- How does a compass work, and why?
- How does an internal combustion engine work?
- How are/were stellar constellations used for navigation?
- Why do some places have seasons, when others don't?
- Why were time zones invented?

- What is natural selection?
- How do modern-day, domesticated dogs compare with their wolf ancestors?
- What are dominant traits, and how do they work?
- How do planes fly?
- What is the history of flight?
- What would you need to be able to survive on the planet Mars?
- What are the main similarities and differences between humans and apes?
- How did the Industrial Revolution affect the environment?
- What alternative energy sources are being developed?
- How do plants turn sunlight into food?

Geography

- What are plate tectonics and how have they influenced the world's geography?
- How have African countries' names and borders changed over history?
- Why are English and French spoken in many places in Africa?
- How did the fall of the Iron Curtain affect Europe's geography?
- Who was the first person to explore the South Pole?
- How did Lewis and Clark explore the Louisiana Purchase?
- What was the history surrounding the largest single acquisition of land in the history of the United States?
- Who, besides Christopher Columbus, is reputed to have discovered the North American continent, and under what historical circumstances?
- How does population density affect living conditions?
- What is the Continental Divide, and where is it?
- Why do all rivers in North America run from North to South?
- How did the current Interstate Highway system come about?

Government

- What is the importance of the electoral college?
- How does the structure of the United States government compare with those of other countries?

- What are the main responsibilities of the president of the United States?
- What officers are included in the president's cabinet, and what are their duties?
- Which U.S. presidents have been related to other U.S. presidents?
- What are the differences between a monarchy and a dictatorship?
- Under what historical circumstances was "the right to bear arms" established?
- What is parliamentary procedure, and how does it work?
- How did Social Security come into being?
- How does the system of "checks and balances" between the three branches of the federal government work, and why is it important?

Economics

- What is capitalism?
- What is socialism?
- How does capitalism compare to socialism?
- How does the economy affect the unemployment rate?
- What circumstances brought about the Great Depression?
- How did World War II bring America out of the Great Depression?
- Is it possible that America would ever have another Great Depression?
- What is a monopoly?
- What is an entrepreneur?
- How does the concept of supply and demand work?

15 Creative Writing

IN THE VAST majority of elementary schools, most writing assignments involve the creation of stories. The emphasis of the teacher is initially on the mechanics of capitalization, punctuation, spelling, and grammar. In time, student writers also explore the elements of fiction, including characters, setting, and plot. However, creative writing has the potential to involve much more than telling a story and developing characters and plot lines. The best creative writing delights our senses, challenges our minds, and engages a broad range of emotional reactions, including love and anger, sadness and joy, contempt and empathy. When our students are engaged in creative writing, the question that careful readers must ask is not merely, What are you trying to say? but also, What are you feeling and how do you want the reader to feel?

DELIGHTING THE SENSES

In encouraging students to be excellent creative writers, we must first help them to see their words through the eyes of the reader. First, we can ask what the reader sees. Each word helps to paint a picture of the images and movements in the story.

> The girl was wearing a red dress the color of Valentine's Day hearts, a color that reminded her that once each year everyone in the class had to be nice to everyone else.

Note that the description did not improve because the writer went to a thesaurus and found a long word to replace a short one. Using the same three-letter adjective, *red,* the writer made associations that described with absolute clarity the specific shade of red that she had in mind. Moreover, her careful use of association to enrich the description allowed the reader to get some insight into the reason that this particular red is more than just a primary color.

The other senses of hearing, touch, smell, and taste are equally important to a complete description of character, event, or setting. As is the case with visual images, the writer can use associations to convey extra meaning. For example, in describing a trip to a fast-food restaurant, the writer might include this detail about smell.

> When we walked to the restaurant, I could smell the burgers frying before I could see the sign. Most people don't like that smell, but it reminds me of walking to a special meal, just my father and me. I don't really like fast food that much. The smells of flowers or chicken soup are much nicer. But I loved those walks and the fatty odors from that restaurant where we would share stories and my dad would listen to me—just me.

Students need not fill their sentences with rhetorical flourishes for their words to have power. They certainly do not need to express themselves in a florid style that will require their peers and teachers to consult a dictionary just to wade through a paragraph. When writers delight the senses, they do so not with complexity and artificial sophistication, but with words that are simple, clear, and strong.

CHALLENGING THE MIND

Creative writing should challenge the mind as well as delight the senses. Our appetite for the unexpected and our interest in solving a fictional crime explains the popularity of surprise endings by authors such as Guy de Maupassant, O. Henry, and elementary school students. Readers like stories with unexpected endings, so it is no surprise that students enjoy writing them. An unexpected ending is not the only way to challenge the mind, though it is a very good start. The writer should try to get readers to consider several plausible endings and be sufficiently interested in the characters and the possible outcomes of the story that they persist in reading. An excellent way to encourage intellectual engagement is to use realistic settings, historical events, and real characters to tell a story. These devices not only make the writing process more interesting, but also result in writing that is much more believable. When historical figures and settings are employed, students do not need to recreate the life of a character with some fictional insertions. Rather, students can invent a character who is peripheral to a well-known historical event and add events and descriptions that engage the reader in a startling way. Here are some examples of stories about fictional characters that have a factual basis:

"Lincoln's Guard," a story about the man who was responsible for protecting Abraham Lincoln on the day of the assassination.

"Leonardo's Friend," a story about a child befriended by Da Vinci and how the child believed in the fanciful inventions of Leonardo when most adults considered the ideas preposterous.

"The Mother from Mali," a story of a woman on a slave ship who devoted her life in America to finding her own family and helping other children to reunite with their parents.

Each of these stories offers the opportunity for rich description and compelling plots. In addition, the writer will learn details about the lives and times of authentic historical characters. As preparation for the inevitable times when your child complains that "I don't have anything to write about," it is a great idea to keep track of story starters such as these about Lincoln, Leonardo, and a heroic woman from Africa. In casual conversations, students sometimes imagine how historical events and famous characters might have intersected with and affected the lives of others. When you hear those observations, consider writing them down. "That would make a great story someday!" you can say, as one or two sentence fragments are added to a story starter list or idea journal.

EMOTIONAL REACTIONS

One of the most important features of great writing is the emotional engagement of the reader. In Roald Dahl's *Matilda,* we share the precocious girl's frustration with her parents and we laugh at her pranks. In Dahl's *Danny, The Champion of the World,* we seethe with rage at the unfairness of the pheasant hunter and our hearts melt at the bond between Danny and his father. In E. B. White's *Charlotte's Web,* we weep with the entire barnyard at

Charlotte's sacrifice. These exceptional writers are not manipulating the emotions of their readers, but are simply telling stories. The characters are not believable because we accept the literal truth of talking pigs and spiders or girls with special powers. Rather, we find the feelings of these characters not only believable but essentially true. In the case study included in this chapter, you will see the emotions of one young author unfold as she makes the transition from spare descriptions in "The Awful Ski Trip" to her engagement of our emotions as she relates the fear and panic of her main character in "Icicle Tears."

CREATIVE WRITING: A CASE STUDY

Of all the genres of written expression, creative writing is perhaps the least amenable to the advice of outsiders. Creative writers tend to own their characters, while the writer of a research paper is considerably less attached to a subpoint on an outline. Teachers and parents generally take a gentle approach to the reading and criticism of creative writing, not realizing that criticism need not be harsh or negative to be effective. The best way to elicit improvements from creative writers is through sincere questions from readers. Examples of effective questions include:

What do the characters see?
What do the characters hear?
What do the characters smell?
What do the characters touch? How does it feel?
What do the characters taste?
How do you feel about each of the characters?
How do you want the reader to feel about them?

POETRY: THE DANCE OF WORDS

Webster's Dictionary defines poetry as "writing that formulates a concentrated imaginative awareness of experience in language chosen and arranged to create a specific emotional response through meaning, sound, and rhythm." Because of the breathtaking variety of poetry, children respond to the challenge of writing it in a multitude of ways. Some children find their poetic voice in rhythm, others in rhyme, and others in open verse. When the poetic form has very specific requirements, such as haiku or sonnets, artistic expression must conform to a strict set of rules. Although some might view more formalistic writing as somehow restrictive, in fact, it requires a good deal of creative thought to satisfy both the young poet and the form's demands. When the poetic form is unstructured, students are free to play with words, form, style—even how the poem is printed out. Regardless of the form of a poem, however, students use language quite differently in poetry than in prose. Words can be repeated for emphasis, or phrases and expressions can be repeated, like the chorus of a song. The poet may inform, as a descriptive writer does, but poets have an emotional agenda. Although the meaning of words is important to the poet, the sound and rhythm of the words are as integral to the poem as their definitions.

Student writers frequently write about nature, animals, and the environment. Your invitation to write in poetic form allows your child to move from the sentence, "I like rainbows" to Wordsworth's opening line, "My heart leaps up when I behold a rainbow in the sky." The invitation to touch on raw emotion allows your child to embrace the final line of the stanza, "So let it be when I grow old, or let me die." The rhyme is icing on the cake. The same Mr. Hillier who provided the meticulous editing described in chapter 9 always recited these words with a quiver in his voice. In five lines of verse, he recalled the rainbows of his youth and defined his reason for tolerating the challenges of old age. When he gave voice to Wordsworth's words, his heart did leap up, and so did ours. Poetry, whether about nature, love, joy, or sorrow, goes to the heart.

Anger is as powerful an emotion as joy, and the rhythm of poetry provides the perfect expression for the writer who wishes to pound, pound, pound on the bedroom wall. Elementary students can read poetry from Steinberg to Shakespeare to find the voice for their angry tears and frustrations ready to explode. With tragic outbreaks of violence in schools and the world at large, parents may be reluctant to encourage writing that reflects anger and revenge. We cannot choose whether our children have these feelings, but we can influence the manner in which those feelings are explored and expressed. Poetry, even when shouted, is preferable to violence. The rage remains, but the expression is different. We cannot take back a wild punch, but we can hone words to a fine point. This substitution of poetic assaults for physical ones is good advice for all students. Giving them imperatives to "Behave!" and "Get along!" are, to most kids, the mindlessness typical of adults who do not understand their lives. Giving students the opportunity to be angry, sad, and aggrieved acknowledges the truth of their feelings and provides a less destructive means of expression.

THE IMPORTANCE OF POETRY IN THE HOME

I do not know of a single state test that requires students to write poetry, but there are many state examinations that require personal narratives or essays that are descriptive, persuasive, or analytical. When I recently asked an elementary student, "Do you ever write poetry in school?" she answered, "No—we don't have the time." In Elizabeth's classroom, poetry is an unimportant frill. As you consider the potential benefits of writing poetry for elementary school children, ask yourself whether the time devoted to finding the right word, rhythm, and meaning would be wasted.

The best way to start your child on the journey of writing poetry is to read good poetry aloud together. This will take time, and it may surprise you. While Shel Silverstein and e. e. cummings are staples among children's poets, the words of Maya Angelou, Shakespeare, Wordsworth, and Dickinson may ignite the poet in your child. The journey from reading to writing poetry begins with a single stanza. Let your child read a few lines and then take turns. Experiment with different accents, rhythms, and syllables for emphasis. Try different voices, ranging from soft to loud, feminine to masculine.

A sentence in a poem about a subject that deeply affects the poet can include the typical subject and verb, with perhaps an adjective thrown in, or that same thought can be embellished with the poetic use of rhythm and sound. In this way, "the ringing bell" becomes Edgar Allan Poe's "tintinnabulation that so musically wells from the bells, bells, bells." Reading poetry aloud together will introduce your child to the musical potential of words.

THE ROOTS OF POETRY: MUSIC AND ART

The search for detail in music and art can serve as an important inspiration for writers of all ages. Although a typical classroom assignment may ask students to listen to a particularly vivid piece of music such as Stravinsky's *Firebird,* a better task is to allow your child to listen to three different orchestras play the piece and notice the similarities and differences. Just as the notes of the composer vary widely from the interpretation of one musician to another, the words of the poet are dramatically affected by the pace and intonation of the reader. Encourage your child to play with the sound of the words, reading quickly and slowly, in martial rhythms and jazz syncopations, in loud declamation and soft understatement.

Detail in art will also help your child move from ideas to their final expression. Two recognizable examples are Rodin's *The Thinker* and Monet's *Water Lilies.* Your child may recognize these famous works of art, but may not realize that Rodin and Monet created multiple drawings, paintings, and sculptures of these two works, each with significant differences. The difference in the placement of the Thinker's hand or in the clarity of the lily's leaf say a great deal about the artwork. They are small details, but from such small details significant differences in interpretation and understanding will spring. In a poem, a single word or the decision on where that word belongs in proximity to other words form crucial distinctions for the poet and the reader.

The next time you take your child to an art museum, resist the temptation to view every work in the place and say, as my mother heard someone remark about their visit to the Louvre, "We only had four hours, but I think we saw it all." Instead, consider finding only two works. If chairs are available, sit down with your child, relax, and just think about the art. Find a detail that was not obvious at first, and then find another detail, and yet another. You need not take your child to Paris to treasure such moments of discovery. Some of the least crowded art exhibits are those of your local art club. Kids tend to be remarkably frank about art, and artists are willing to endure the occasional criticism in order to hear a child's completely genuine "That's amazing!"

 TYPES OF POETRY

Listed below are several major types of poetry, the characteristics that set them apart, and examples of each. You and your child can easily spend an afternoon looking up examples of different types of poems and trying your hand at using the forms to create your own poems. A great resource for poetry of all types is *The Norton Anthology of Poetry* (Norton, 1996).

Haiku

Haiku is a form of poetry developed by the Japanese. The title of the poem also serves as the first line, and the poem is only three lines long. The first line consists of five syllables, the second of seven, and the third of five. The subject matter is often nature. *Example:* Ezra Pound's "In a Station of the Metro."

Student example:

Spring

Apple tree in bloom.
White flakes of snow fall on it.
Is this really spring?

Iambic Pentameter

Iambic pentameter is not actually a poetic form, although it can be used inside other forms. It is a meter. The word *iamb* refers to a pair of syllables, one of which is unstressed, the other stressed. The *penta* in *pentameter* refers to the number five (as in pentagram or pentagon), so that iambic pentameter is one line of five iambs. It is often used in sonnets, below.

Sonnet

Sonnets have, of course, been made famous by William Shakespeare, but there are other forms. All sonnets have fourteen lines of iambic pentameter. What sets a Shakespearean (or English) sonnet apart from an Italian sonnet is the rhyme scheme. Assuming that each letter refers to a rhyming couplet (a pair of words that rhyme, like "day" and "way"), the structure of a Shakespearean sonnet is as follows:

A
B
A
B

C
D
C
D

E
F
E
F

G
G

Notice that the only rhyme that does not alternate with another rhyme is the last one. The rhyme scheme of an Italian sonnet is slightly different:

A
B
B
A

A
B
B
A

C
D
E

C
D
E

Examples: Shakespearean Sonnet: William Shakespeare's "Shall I Compare Thee to a Summer's Day?" (Sonnet XVIII). Italian Sonnet: John Milton, "When I Consider How My Light Is Spent."

Quatrain

Quatrain is a great form to use just to practice rhyming. You can use any meter you want, as long as there are four lines in each verse and the ends of the second and fourth lines rhyme (the rhyme scheme would be ABCB). A quatrain poem can consist of just one verse (four lines), or as many as you want. This form is also called ballad stanza, and if you look at the song lyrics, you'll find that many use this form.

Examples: The nursery rhyme "Little Boy Blue"; Samuel Taylor Coleridge's "The Rime of the Ancient Mariner"; Clement C. Moore's "A Visit from St. Nicholas" (more popularly known as "'Twas the Night Before Christmas").

Student example:

Lunch

My mom is always packing lunches
For me and my big brother.
He always wants to trade his sandwich
For something or other.

I would give him my candy bar
Or anything I had
Except his sandwich is always baloney
And I think it tastes really bad.

Acrostic

The first letters of each line of an acrostic poem form a vertical word which usually determines the subject matter for the poem itself.

Example: Bert Kaempfert and Milt Gabler's big-band hit "L-O-V-E," recorded by Nat "King" Cole in 1964.

Student example:

Spring

Pretty little flowers
I see outside my window
Nicely opening up but
Knowing they will soon go.

Limerick

The limerick style is Irish in origin, and limericks are fun to compose. They are five lines long and their meter and rhyme scheme are as follows:

A (8 SYLLABLES)
A (8 SYLLABLES)
B (5 SYLLABLES)

B (5 SYLLABLES)
A (8 SYLLABLES)

Example: Edward Lear wrote many limericks such as "There Was an Old Man with a Beard," though he is better known for his silly poem "The Owl and the Pussycat."
Student example:

A Mouse

Today I walked into my house
And saw on the floor a small mouse.
"Go away!" I cried,
As I ran back outside
Before it could jump on my blouse.

Shaped Poems

These are a fun challenge and often appeal to a child's visually artistic side. They can rhyme or not; the words just have to be in the shape of the subject matter. If a child writes a poem about a flower, the poem has to actually look like a flower. Writing the words with different colored pencils or using colored inks can also add to the visual impact.

Examples: John Hollander's "Swan and Shadow"; Shel Silverstein's "A Poem on the Neck of a Running Giraffe."

Example:

It
Jumped
Out of the water
And just for a second I saw a flash of tiny   fins
And scales, all blue and green and yellow in the bright   light
Arcing and twisting in the air like joy in the making or a line from my
Favorite song. But then it was gone, the surface of the water just
Closing over it like a forgotten dream, only a ripple to   help
Me remember that   it
Was there at
All.

16 The Top Ten Mistakes Parents Make

TO **WRITE** is to be vulnerable. When an author constructs a sentence, it seems, for a moment, to be the perfect conjunction of thought and expression. Later, when that same sentence is read by a stranger, the words may scream of pedantry and foolishness. My students, my friends, and my children have all had the opportunity to find errors, non sequiturs, unsupported assertions, and other assaults on language and logic in my writing. Mistakes are easier to recognize in others than in ourselves. To help our children best, however, we must begin a difficult introspection: a consideration of our own errors. Only after we consider our own errors can we consider the more obvious faults of our kids and their teachers.

THE TOP TEN MISTAKES PARENTS MAKE IN "HELPING" KIDS IMPROVE WRITING

1. "It's not perfect."

It is hard to argue with such a true statement. In fact, if a child combined the talents of Hemingway, Angelou, and Voltaire, the little prodigy would still produce some sentences that were absolutely awful. Perfection is not the standard; proficiency is. We must resist the temptation to highlight every error in syntax and usage. Working one step at a time, we can encourage our children's successes and appropriately note their need for correction.

 2. "Of course it's perfect; it's *my* kid's work!"

A few hours before I wrote these words, I heard five well-meaning, intelligent, and sophisticated parents say that if they were to note all of the errors in their children's work, it would diminish their children's self-esteem. Self-esteem is generally accepted as a good thing. However, the most effective way to foster this quality in our child is not to lie to them and mislead them into believing that their work is splendid when it is in fact deficient. Just as kids know the truth about Santa Claus and the Tooth Fairy long before parents are willing to part with the myths, children also know very well the difference between academic work that merits praise and the more typical good effort, riddled with errors, which receives *pro forma* praise that is neither sincere from the giver nor credible to the recipient. Children learn by being taught. Teaching is, by definition, the imparting of knowledge that is correct and true. When we fail to correct our children's errors, we fail to teach.

3. "You finished! You're done!"

Not really. One of the most valuable gifts we can give to our children is the notion that their first effort is not their last effort. They may indeed be finished with a first draft, but they are not done with the project. Our encouragement, love, and coaching will guide them in the pursuit of continued improvement. Each effort is the next step, not the final step, in their journey to becoming a writer.

4. "That's okay. Some kids just aren't born to be writers."

Just as we parents wish to attribute to our children our own real and imagined skills, we sometimes justify our children's frailties by acknowledging similar weaknesses in ourselves. Even if neither you nor your child is a "natural" writer, diligent work, clear feedback, practice, and multiple opportunities for success can make anyone a writer. The problem is not heredity but the need for hard work.

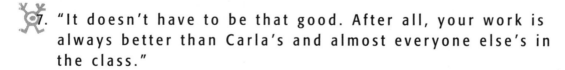5. "Go to your room, do your homework, and don't come out until you are done!"

This command is tempting, and I confess that I have given in to that temptation. However, every time I dispatched a child on a homework mission in a tone that made it sound like solitary confinement, I made a terrible mistake. Sometimes it took many days to repair the damage and reestablish the opportunity for a confident and painless review of homework.

6. "Do you have any homework today, honey?"

After hearing the reassuring "nope," we move on to the next topic of conversation. Here is a good "intellectual hygiene" rule to consider in your house, along the lines of washing one's hands before dinner: Every day is a learning day. Just as we don't skip hand washing on Friday nights, the absence of homework assignments does not eliminate the need for reading, writing, thinking, and other learning activities. Although homework assigned by a teacher surely has a high priority, the absence of assigned homework does not imply that learning activities are prohibited, but only that the learning activities will happen with parents and children. Consider any of the story starters, graphic organizers, or idea generators in this book as a good place to start.

7. "It doesn't have to be that good. After all, your work is always better than Carla's and almost everyone else's in the class."

Children have an acute understanding of the rules by which they are evaluated. Sometimes the standards are objective and clear: They need to get the ball in the goal, or they need to hit each note correctly. The problem with being "better than Carla"—or even better than the rest of the class—is that it is a subjective and ultimately meaningless standard. This information tells children and parents nothing about what a child knows or can do, but provides reassurance that the social and intellectual order remains intact. Your child may be "better than Carla" in many ways and yet not be a proficient reader and writer. Children need to understand from an early age that we create assignments that meet the requirements of the rules, not merely to be a little bit better than others. The standards by which we evaluate student work at home and in schools is no minor educational point. The No Child Left Behind Act, approved by overwhelming majorities in the United States Senate and House of Representatives in 2001 and signed into law in 2002, states unequivocally that every public school in the nation will evaluate students using the academic standards of the states. All of those state standards express the knowledge and skills that students must have to be successful. None of the standards define student success in terms of out-performing other children.

8. "I can't help on that assignment. I'm not even sure that I understand it myself!"

One of the most valuable qualities we can share with our children is the vulnerability of admitting to not knowing the right answer all the time. When we read a set of instructions and sincerely do not understand the teacher's expectations, we get only a glimpse into the daily life of a student. Directions can be unclear, examples misleading, and terminology confusing. In particular, the language of scoring guides and rubrics used in writing assessments can be laden with unfamiliar academic jargon. By approaching these difficulties without the preconception that we adults automatically know all the answers, we join our children on their journey of questioning, frustration, persistence, discovery, and ultimate satisfaction. Along the way, we will make some mistakes. I hope that your mistakes will not be as embarrassing as mine, including the instance in which I evaluated the work of graduate students in statistics without a problem, but provided guidance to my third grader that was flat wrong. Parents who fear that their errant advice will be occasionally corrected by an eight-year-old should savor the intervals between such humiliations; within five years these corrections will become commonplace.

9. "Writing isn't that important; I just want to be sure that my kids can read well."

Although I have heard parents make this argument with some conviction, they are wrong. The evidence and arguments in favor of writing are overwhelming, and the ideas presented in chapter 1 are only the tip of an iceberg of research that supports the importance of writing. In fact, parents who intuitively know the importance of reading for the academic future of their children must consider the impact of the reading-writing connection. If we are to build reading skills successfully, then we must help our children write about what they read, observe, and think.

9. "I don't have the time."

I routinely hear these words from parents. Although I respect the multiple demands for their attention and the sense that something as time consuming as writing must surely be beyond the call of duty, we must confront the fact that the statement, "I don't have the time" is untrue. Unless your day is shorter than twenty-four hours, you have precisely the same amount of time as every parent on the planet. When we say, "I don't have the time," what we really mean, if we are committed to precision in language, is this: "I do have the time to help my child with writing, editing, revising, and improving language skills, but if I spend time on that activity, it will reduce the time I have available for other activities. In fact, some of those other activities are also important for my child. I just can't do it all."

This statement is true. The only issue that remains is whether the time you invest in your child's writing is of greater value than the other activities that crowd the days of busy families. There are three constructive things parents can do to find this elusive time.

First, we must avoid the either/or thinking that the other activities preclude writing. Make it a habit to have an "idea journal" with you when you are traveling to activities or errands. Use the travel time that can be easily consumed by silence or music to listen to your child. Turn off the cell phone, turn off the radio, the Game Boy, unplug the headphones, and listen. Don't settle for monosyllabic responses that typically describe the school day. At the very least, ask your child to read aloud. Of course, the authors to whom you most wish to listen are your children.

Second, limit television time. What is a reasonable limit? Consider this: If your child watches thirty minutes of TV in the morning, a couple of hours after school, and an hour and a half after dinner, as well as three hours in the morning and evening Saturday and Sunday, that is a total of thirty-two hours each week. Astonishingly, that extraordinary expenditure of time is significantly less than many American children spend in front of the television set and more than they spend in school. This discussion is not a commentary about violence, sex, and intellectual dreck on television. Reasonable people can disagree about the quality of available viewing. The incontestable fact is that when kids are watching television they are not interacting with their parents. When parents assert that they "don't have the time" to listen to their children read, ask questions about their writing, or make suggestions for improvement, the truth is that a good portion of the available time has been consumed by television.

Third, we must respond to the challenges of time by making choices. Cancel something. Eliminate just one meeting, resign from a single committee, or discard an activity that has outlived its usefulness. I know of parents and teachers who plan annual "garden parties" with the theme "You can't plant the flowers until you pull the weeds." The flowers represent meaningful activities with children, while the weeds are the time-consuming intrusions that get in the way of our priorities. These parents and teachers know that their devotion to time with children will rest in the wasteland of good intentions unless they first pull some time-wasting weeds. The sheer accumulation of demands in the same school day and fixed number of hours at home has allowed busyness to masquerade as effectiveness. The cycle will not be broken until you pull the first weed.

17 Writing for State Tests

ONE OF THE most perplexing challenges we all face is the gulf between the results of standardized achievement tests and the opinions rendered by teachers and parents about the work of a child. The precocious and enthusiastic reader is adjudged merely "proficient" on a state reading test and, more commonly, the brilliantly creative writer is deemed "below standards." Before succumbing to the impulse to shoot the messenger—the teacher, the test administrator, the state department of education, or the creator of the test—consider what accounts for the difference between your estimation of a child's work and the official judgment of the test. The most likely reason for such a difference is that each observer is evaluating completely different qualities. Where the parent values creativity, the state test values adherence to convention. Where the parent is enthralled with inventiveness, the state requires respect for rules. Rather than debate the merits of each point of view, let us consider that both have merit. Students need the freedom to be original and creative and, at the same time, they need to learn how to apply standard literary conventions.

SIMILARITIES AND DIFFERENCES AMONG STATE WRITING REQUIREMENTS

States vary widely in their requirements for student writing. Appendix C provides a list of states that test writing at the elementary level. Of course, it is important to note that even if your state does not have a formal writing assessment now, a growing number of states and school systems are including writing in their literacy proficiency standards. In addition, middle school and high school writing requirements are growing in number every year. It is not unusual for private schools and selective public schools to require writing samples from prospective students. This chapter provides valuable information about how formal writing is evaluated in large-scale tests.

HOW ARE STUDENTS EVALUATED ON STATE WRITING TESTS?

The official answer that testing officials provide to questions about evaluation is that they use the writing standards established by the state. In practice, however, the application of those standards to evaluation can be remarkably different from what a parent reading the standards might expect. The language of the standards can be rather daunting; for example, in Massachusetts, students in grades three and four are expected to "Write brief summaries of information gathered through research" (Massachusetts English Language Arts Standard 19.12). This seems reasonable, but parents might want more detail about the quality or length of the expected writing. Whatever the language of your state standards, the scoring guide, or scoring rubric, is the key to understanding the expectations your child must meet. The scoring guide is the set of specific rules used by evaluators to identify which student work is proficient and which student work is not. To continue the Massachusetts example, the scoring guide makes clear that a student paper does not have to be perfect in order to receive a "proficient" score of 3 (on a 1-to-4 point scale). But, according to the scoring guide, it is imperative that the student's errors "do not interfere with communication," or that there be "few relative to the length of the essay . . ." California academic content standards are clear, specific, and almost overwhelming to many teachers and students. But a review of the scoring guide used to assess the fourth-grade writing test reveals a more reasonable approach. As in Massachusetts, a 1- to 4-point scale is used, and a proficient score of 3 "contains some errors in the conventions of the English language (grammar, punctuation, capitalization, and spelling). These errors do **not** interfere with the reader's understanding of the writing."

USING WRITING SCORING GUIDES AT SCHOOL AND AT HOME

The scoring guides offer essential information for students, teachers, and parents. These devices allow us to provide specific feedback that will both encourage and challenge a student. Because the scoring guides typically include multiple dimensions of evaluation, such as organization, mechanics, and style, it is possible to give a student sincere encouragement about the strongest part of her essay while pointing out other, weaker elements. A student who receives a nonproficient score may be tempted to wad up the paper, throw it away, start over, and then make precisely the same mistakes again. When a student becomes accustomed to using a scoring guide, she can preserve the best parts of her writing and then proceed to the next draft to work on specific corrections. Our coaching must be incremental. Using a comprehensive writing rubric, you might find twenty-five things wrong with your child's essay. But as you work on improving each draft, it is wise to limit your comments to no more than two or three areas of focus. At the same time, it is almost always possible to find some parts of the essay to praise.

When providing feedback to your child, it's best to focus on content first, followed by spelling and legibility, mechanics, and grammar. The questions below will help you guide your child through the revision process.

1. Content

   Why is that?
   What else do you know about this?
   Can you give me some more details? It's really interesting! Please tell me more about it.

2. Clarification (spelling and legibility)

   I don't understand that word—what word is that?
   I can't tell where one sentence starts and the other one begins—can you help me?
   I can't figure out what this letter is—could you write it more neatly for me?

3. Mechanics

Does every sentence start with a capital letter? Let's check.

Does every sentence end with the right punctuation mark? Please show me.

Is this comma used correctly?

4. Grammar

The most common error is subject-verb agreement. For example, "They was going to the park." Rather than circle the error, consider this technique:

"Would you read this sentence aloud? How does it sound to you?"

At this point, many grammatical errors will be evident, particularly if the student is accustomed to hearing English spoken correctly. If this doesn't work, try:

"When you write the word 'they,' how many people are you taking about? Four people? Is it OK if I say, 'Four people was going to the park?' "

If necessary, remind your child that plural subjects require plural verbs. It is much better, however, if the student hears examples that are correct, identifies examples that are correct, and then corrects the mistake.

Consider Josie's response to this prompt on a practice state writing exam:

Write about a famous person who has been an influence on you. Support your answer with details and examples.

Third grader Josie decided to write about Theodore Roosevelt and provided the following first draft:

I admire President Theodore Roosevelt. He was a president. He started Yellowstone National Park. He liked nature, and that's why they named the Teddy Bear after him. He had a Bull Moose party. Well, that's about all I know about Theodore Roosevelt.

Josie's writing, if we were only to consider penmanship, punctuation, grammar, and spelling, is perfect. Every sentence has a period and begins with a capital letter. Every sentence has a subject and verb. Every word is spelled correctly. Nevertheless, this paper is likely to receive a very low rating on a state test because it does not respond to the question. Students of all ages prefer to write within their comfort zone, telling what they know, rather than responding directly to the question. The perennial challenge is to learn to write to the question, which always demands something more. If we are to give Josie feedback on this first draft, we must be specific and constructive. One of the best techniques for helping students to link the feedback to the question is to allow them to read their essay, then read the question, and then respond aloud to the writing prompt slightly rephrased. For example, after listening to her essay, I would ask Josie, "Why are *you* so interested in Teddy Roosevelt?" The missing link in her response is that she did not talk about how the subject of the essay had influenced her. She gave a few details about the president, but no details at all about how the president's life had influenced her own. As Josie answers this question, I would ask her to start making a list, which will become the source for an eventual web or other pre-writing organizational device.

Finally, before Josie begins her second draft, I would offer some very specific coaching: "Josie, your handwriting is beautiful! I also noticed that you spelled every word, including *Roosevelt* correctly. The writing prompt asks you to tell about a famous person who has been an influence on you. That means you are part of this essay. You tell us a lot about Teddy Roosevelt and who he was, but I want to learn how he influenced you. In the next draft, please tell me more about that. By the way, I also noticed that every sentence began with a capital letter—that's perfect!"

CREATING YOUR OWN SCORING GUIDES

Sometimes the scoring guides used in state tests (and, for that matter, those used in elementary classrooms) are complex and difficult to understand. If the scoring guide you are attempting to use with your child is not working well, don't complain to the state. Fix the scoring guide. I am not suggesting that you ignore the state writing requirements, but rather that you translate those requirements into language that is accessible to your child. Appendix C includes an example of a "student-friendly" scoring guide.

A paper whose author would qualify as "Stage 6—The Extending Writer" on the Georgia Third-Grade Writing Assessment must possess the following characteristics:

- A topic that is fully elaborated with rich details.
- Organization that sustains the writer's purpose and moves the reader through the piece.

- Audience awareness techniques that engage and sustain the reader's interest.
- Effective use of varied sentence patterns.
- Creative and novel language.
- Errors in surface features that do not interfere with the reader's understanding of the writer's message.

I asked one third grader whose reading skills are advanced several years beyond his current grade level what these criteria mean. He replied honestly, "I don't know." Within the past week, I was asked by a group of angry parents, including a school board member who had studied the issue with some interest, why so many children in that area were told that they were "good writers" by their teachers and then received low scores on the state test. The problem is not incompetent teachers or indolent children, but rather that writing is evaluated quite differently on state tests than it is in most classrooms. Writing is almost never evaluated at home the way that it is on state tests. Even if we tried to do so, we could confront requirements such as "audience awareness techniques that engage and sustain the reader's interest" and still have very little idea of what this means when it comes to coaching a third grader to improve her writing. Therefore, we, along with our children, must create our own rules for great writing. These will form a mental checklist that, regardless of the writing task, allows you and your child to use a common vocabulary to evaluate the quality of a piece of writing. Here is just one example that some elementary school students developed and, after rearranging the sequence, gave the acronym QUIET.

Q—Question: Did I answer the question in the test?
U—Understand: Can I understand what I just wrote? Are the letters neat and the ideas clear?
I—Interest: Is it interesting, with great details and examples?
E—Errors: Did I check for correct spelling, capitalization, punctuation, and grammar?
T—Topic: Does the first sentence tell about the rest of the essay? Does that lead to a clear beginning, middle, and end?

REQUIREMENTS COMMON IN ALL STATES

Although the requirements for elementary writing range from summaries of text to analysis of characters in a story to narratives of personal experiences to persuasive essays, there are some common characteristics of student writing that virtually every state requires. These requirements may not match the official writing requirements of your state, but they are common characteristics of the writing that earns high scores on state tests. Interestingly, the same characteristics have been found to be related to higher scores on high school essays and law school finals. The characteristics are: legibility, organization, and length.

Legibility

Your third-grade teacher was right: neatness counts. The counterarguments are familiar. Your doctor has horrible handwriting and is successful nevertheless. This is the twenty-first century and everyone types. We have voice-recognition software and one need only dictate into the end of an electronic pen. The fact is that the vast majority of state writing tests require students to write (usually by hand) a response so that a human scorer can read it. The human scorers are frequently admonished that "neatness does not count," yet I have never met the human scorer who can evaluate writing he or she cannot read. Moreover, every state writing guide has a code for "illegible" or "not able to score," and therefore the practical requirement for penmanship is clear. The human scorer considers neither intention nor attitude, only the images on the page. It is not antiquarian inappropriateness for parents to insist on good penmanship. It still matters. If your child cannot write cursive in a legible manner, then it is acceptable to print on state tests. When printing, children should use upper and lower case rather than block capital letters so that the scorers are able to understand which capital letters are intentional and not mark the paper down for capitalization errors.

Organization

Every essay requires a beginning, a middle, and an end. Whether the requirement is for a personal narrative, literary analysis, or persuasive essay, the writer must have a clear idea of structure. The best way to accomplish this is through the use of a graphic organizer or an outline (chapter 7). In the instructions accompanying writing prompts on some state tests, students are expected to take time for pre-writing activities, including outlines, webs, or other graphic organizers. Even in those cases where the student is simply given a prompt and some blank, lined pages, there is invariably some scratch paper or unfilled area in the test materials that the student can use to organize the essay. When students write without planning, they tend to give answers that are aimless and poorly sequenced. When students take time to write an outline, even if the scorer never sees that outline, the essay created by the student will be better organized and that will lead to a higher score.

Length

Teachers from elementary school through college conduct an intricate tap dance when confronted with the question, "How long does my paper have to be?" With practiced evasions such as, "Long enough to cover the subject," we fail to give students concrete guidelines. Although I understand the risk of inappropriate generalization and the need to consider each topic individually, I also understand how maddening it is to kids when adults fail to respond to reasonable inquiries. More important, in reviewing actual student writing in elementary classrooms, I find that a large amount of writing is limited to sentence fragments in reply to questions on worksheets. Occasionally, several sentences are used to provide an "extended response," and on rare occasions students are expected to create full paragraphs, including a topic sentence and, of course, editing, revision, and rewriting. Exceedingly rare is the elementary classroom where students are routinely creating three- to five-paragraph essays. This requirement occurs even more rarely in the home. Unfortunately, that is the very reason otherwise bright and capable students are unprepared for state writing tests. They do not lack the ability or interest; they simply never had the opportunity to practice on a consistent basis meeting the expectations of those tests.

Here is my unofficial guidance about length of elementary school essays on state tests:

Grades 1 and 2: Five to seven sentences in one paragraph.

Grade 3 and 4: Three paragraphs, each paragraph having about five sentences.

Grade 5: Five paragraphs, each paragraph having about five sentences, with the exception of the brief opening and closing paragraphs, which may have only three or four sentences.

I offer these guidelines because ambiguity invites confusion and frustration. If your state would have evaluated a four-paragraph essay from a fifth grader as perfectly satisfactory, there is little risk when a student provides five. But if your child has never practiced writing essays of this length—and I know of many classrooms where that is the case—then the guidelines may spur you to provide supplementary writing opportunities at home.

WHAT ABOUT "COMPUTER-SCORED" ESSAY TESTS?

A new trend that was regarded as science fiction only a decade ago is rapidly becoming a fixture in the scoring of essay tests. That is the use of computer-scored tests, sometimes inaccurately called "artificial intelligence" programs. According to officials at the College Board and Vantage Learning, two organizations that have formed a partnership for automated scoring of essay exams, over five million student essay tests have already been evaluated by computers. Before the end of 2002, the number of computer-scored tests is expected to exceed fourteen million. At this point, these computer-scored tests require students to type their essays on a computer keyboard. As a result, they are typically only used by older students. The quality of the scoring of computer-graded essays is good, comparing favorably to the typical situation in which the same essay is scored independently by two raters. The quality of computer scoring is typically higher than that of a single human scorer, if "quality" is evaluated in terms of consistency with the state standard and scoring guide. Of course, what a computer does not provide is the encouragement, coaching, and specific feedback that a parent or teacher can. The human scorers now involved in large-scale state writing tests are not providing much in the way of feedback, with a few notable examples such as Massachusetts, where the student may receive specific recommendations for improvement and specific commendations on an essay. Unfortunately, this feedback comes to the student months after the test is over.

As recently as 2001, I would have been tempted to dismiss the future of computer-scored writing tests for elementary school students. For reasons elaborated in chapter 8, I continue to believe that penmanship still matters and that the physical properties of paper, envelopes, and books cannot be replaced by microchips. Nevertheless, a combination of cost controls and reliability requirements will undoubtedly lead some states to extend their experimentation with machine scoring from the upper grades to the elementary level, at least with regard to expensive large-scale testing. Thus, while the need for penmanship will not be replaced by keyboarding skills, the development of competent keyboarding techniques by elementary school students is clearly a basic skill of the twenty-first century.

SAMPLE SCORING GUIDES

Appendix B provides sample scoring guides for several state writing tests, including California, Colorado, Florida, North Carolina, and Texas. If your state tests writing at the elementary level, I encourage you to ask your child's teacher how the standards outlined in the state's writing rubric are applied in class and how the school prepares students for the writing test. If your state does not have a writing test, your child's teacher should still provide students with a clear set of expectations. Principals or teachers should provide you with a written, clear, and specific scoring rubric, even if it is locally developed rather than an official state document. Parents have the right to know what students are expected to learn and how they will be expected to demonstrate their knowledge and skills. In the case of student writing, the teacher should describe the characteristics of satisfactory writing and unsatisfactory writing in explicit terms.

Whatever the format of the documents in your child's school, make sure you review the applicable rubric with your child, working together to convert jargon into terms you and your child understand.

18 Developing the Habit of Writing

SOME CHILDREN express themselves in writing as naturally as other children sing, play, or dance. For other children, the words come slowly and with hesitation. For them, writing is an insufficiently rewarding chore, with the effort barely worth the occasional praise. Even for enthusiastic writers, the commitment to writing excellence will wax and wane, diminishing with changes in mood and circumstance. As parents, our task is to encourage the reluctant writer and to spur the prolific writer on to greater bursts of creativity. Here are seven practical things every parent can do to help children develop the habit of writing.

1. Maintain a well-stocked supply cabinet.

Paper (lined and unlined), pencils, pens, poster boards, graph paper, and colored paper should be easy to find and always on hand. For students using word processors, always keep an extra ink cartridge available (though it might be a good idea if the installation is a job performed only with parental supervision). In addition to these typical school supplies, consider some special writing supplies that reflect the individual taste of each child. Let your child pick out some special paper that can be used for party invitations, notes, or special projects. Have pencils of varying thicknesses and pens of different colors. Just as you want your child to develop a sense of ownership of the words on the page, you can also promote a proprietary feeling about the accoutrements of writing.

2. Give your child a diary or journal.

The ones that my children have enjoyed most have two important characteristics beyond the cover and paper—their name and a lock. Writing is personal, and their diaries are private. While young children will likely want to share their writings with you at some point, that must be their decision. The purpose in giving the gift is to convey a sense of trust in their power to commit their thoughts to paper. Over time, this gift may become a tradition, with each birthday or holiday reminding you that it is time for another journal. Too soon the cartoon characters will give way to leather binding, but the sentiment remains the same with each gift. You are telling your child, "You are a writer, and I love you."

3. Give your child personalized stationery.

This gift can be a gentle prelude to the requirement for thank-you notes for every gift as well as the tradition of weekly letters to grandparents or other relatives. You can create personalized stationery on a computer, but make the effort to use a special paper, a distinctive typeface, and matching envelopes. Be sure to enclose a book of postage stamps bearing an image that is unusual and special.

4. Write notes to your child and encourage him to write to you.

These need not be elaborate epistles. I have put Post-it Notes in lunch boxes and been lucky enough to receive notes secretly tucked in my briefcase in return. Although most families use commercial cards for birthdays and holidays, always take the time to fill the white space with your personal sentiments and make it a family tradition to linger over the cards and handwritten expressions in them before ripping the wrapping off of the present.

4. Keep a family bulletin board.

The refrigerator door is the traditional display venue for student work, but it is rarely large enough to contain many examples of student writing. A bulletin board or perhaps several adhesive cork tiles will serve as a splendid display of your child's work. It is particularly encouraging to notice the progression over time from the first captions of pictures before kindergarten to the essays of growing sophistication throughout elementary school.

5. Immerse your child in the great writing of others.

You should start building your child's lifetime library right now. Contemporary and classic literature, from this year's Newberry Award winners to the Winnie the Pooh stories of A. A. Milne, will form the foundation of one of the most important gifts you will ever give to your child. A recent news article featuring interviews with first-year college students observed that, although only a few of the accumulations of a young lifetime would fit into the typical college dormitory room, every single one of the students interviewed included several prized children's books among the possessions so valuable that they made the trip to college.

6. Publish and collect your child's writing.

A number of bookstores and schools sponsor activities in which children can publish their own books and then hold a public reading of their work. Bookbinding supplies are inexpensive and easily available from most office supply stores. The act of publication conveys the important message that your child's writing has an audience and, most important, that your child is a real writer. Publication shows that the drawings, words, and ideas are not merely abstract exercises, but the acts of an author with a message, a story, and thoughts worthy of discovery by others.

There is another reason for beginning the collection of your child's published works. When the day comes for your child to leave for college with a few of the treasured books you've given her, you will also have a collection of treasured volumes authored by your child. My oldest child, Brooks, to whom this book is dedicated, is now in college writing plays, short stories, analytical essays, and cartoons. Not far from his latest literary creations on my desk is a copy of the story for which he won his first Young Author's prize in second grade, "The Real True Story of Noah's Ark." My collection is filled with his elementary-school writing and includes art that would probably embarrass him now, as it contains his first "Binnie the Bear" cartoons and the first play that he produced, *An Inspector Calls*. This collection offers early glimpses of his humor, intelligence, and passion. Along with every parent who has ever sent a child to college, I miss him desperately even as I delight in his newfound independence. I am lucky to have *The Collected Works of Brooks Reeves* as my literary companion.

19 Writing Tools

TRADITIONAL WRITING tools can be intimidating for children. Heavy dictionaries with tiny print are often overwhelming. While almanacs and encyclopedias are fascinating, they are frequently too voluminous for children to explore independently. On the other hand, children quickly outgrow the early dictionaries with many pictures but few words that they do not already know. This chapter offers some ideas for print and electronic resources that help young writers stretch beyond the first dictionaries but stop well short of the *Oxford English Dictionary.* In addition, we will look at other resources that may be helpful to a child struggling to find just the right word or a supporting statistic or fact. I'll also discuss how to access the resources of the Internet in a manner appropriate for elementary students.

The first resource your child should master is the dictionary. The *DK Merriam-Webster Children's Dictionary* (New York: Dorling Kindersley, 2000) provides child-friendly definitions and helpful illustrations. For very young children, consider *Scholastic First Dictionary* (Judith Levey, ed., New York: Scholastic, 1998). Another alternative for children of any age is the creation of their own dictionary. Depending on the grade level, their dictionary may include not only primary definitions, but also parts of speech and examples of the words in sentences. This is a great summertime project in which children "collect words" in the same way they might accumulate rocks or coins. Each word should be placed on a note card, and then the contents of the card can be expanded, with definitions, pronunciations, illustrations, and examples of the appropriate use of the word in a sentence. Eventually the cards can be arranged in alphabetical order and assembled into a book.

One of the most important developments in a child's vocabulary is the ability to express an idea in different ways, noticing not only the similar meanings but also the subtle differences between words like *great, fantastic,* and *wonderful* or *thin, skinny,* and *slim. The American Heritage Children's Thesaurus* (Paul Hellweg, Boston: Houghton Mifflin, 1997) is an excellent assembly of synonyms. The classic *Roget's Thesaurus* is also available in a range of sizes well short of the collegiate editions. While some teachers discourage the use of a thesaurus as a crutch, I would argue that for young writers who enjoy playing with language and learning new words, the thesaurus plays a valuable role. Moreover, it is faster and easier for children to expand their vocabularies when they are learning several words with a single association rather than the same number of unrelated words.

An important component of descriptive, analytical, and persuasive essays is the use of examples, statistics, and facts. *The World Almanac for Kids 2003* (Elaine Israel, ed., New York: World Almanac Education, 2003) is a useful tool. (A new edition is published annually in August.) If your family enjoys trivia games on long trips or after dinner, this resource can also be the great equalizer between older and younger siblings as well as between parents and children, with the smallest child maintaining custody of the almanac while the older competitors rely on memory.

Children's poetry is wonderful, even when the word choices are a bit forced due to the constraints of rhyme and structure. One useful resource is *The Scholastic Rhyming Dictionary* (Sue Young, New York: Scholastic, 1997). Much of children's poetry is dominated by the use of the acrostic, in which the only requirement is the use of the first letter of the theme of the word (*MOTHER* is likely to begin with *mother, mom, my mom* or perhaps with a little more searching, *marvelous* or *magnificent.* Equipped with a rhyming dictionary, your child might be more willing to tackle a poetic form that requires strict rhyme and meter. Elementary students can write sonnets and, with access to the right tools, your child may one day surprise you with a sonnet in the best Mother's Day card you've ever received.

In addition to reference books, there are a growing number of resources available on the Web. A word of warning to parents about using the Internet as a resource for young writers. I intended to list some helpful Web sites here, including several that have been enthusiastically endorsed by parents and children. Indeed, I had personally reviewed several of the sites only a few months ago. Shortly before this book went to press, a colleague reviewed the Web sites again and found one in particular to be not only poorly administered and unhelpful, but grossly inappropriate. The problem with some Web sites for young writers is that the original concept was excellent but proved not sustainable over time. Some sites, for example, seek to provide a forum in which young writers can share their creative efforts and receive feedback on their writing. Sometimes this works well, and participating students are enthusiastic about the availability of abundant feedback and readers who appear to take their writing seriously. The open architecture of such a Web site, however, allows anyone to masquerade as a student reader and strike up an E-mail correspondence with your child. Moreover, the postings of the writers are not reviewed for language or content, and on an otherwise helpful site, my colleague found both language and scenes that were inappropriate for an elementary school student. Rather than risk a recommendation that I would want to retract, I will provide a general word of caution: If your child expresses an interest in an online forum for student writers—one recommended by a teacher or friend, or mentioned in an article in a children's magazine—be sure to visit the site regularly yourself and monitor your child's online visits.

20 Putting This Book into Practice

WHAT NOW? You know that writing is one of the most effective ways to build your child's thinking, reasoning, and communications skills. You know that it is very likely that the typical elementary school curriculum will omit some elements of writing that are essential for preparing your child for secondary school. And you know that you have the ability and information necessary to help your child succeed. This chapter offers some guidelines for adapting this book to the unique needs of your child.

Although writing plays an increasingly important role in student success on state tests, the real rationale for your encouragement of writing by your child is the nurturing of lifelong skills that will provide benefits outside the classroom. Beyond the practical benefits in secondary school, college, and the job market are the joys that await the young writer who strikes up an engaging correspondence with a relative or friend, influences the actions of others through persuasive writing, or thrills to see his or her name on a published document. If the ideas in this book become a list of dreary chores, I fear that I have failed you. If, by contrast, your child can help you leaf through the pages, find an interesting idea, and try something new, fun, and challenging, then my hopes for the reader have been fulfilled. As a teacher and parent, I have seen the good intentions of parents equipped with helpful books and manuals fall short of the mark. Here are some ideas to help you get the most out of this book.

TAKE SMALL STEPS

Rather than take a student through the entire writing process, consider the use of a single graphic organizer and then take a break. Rather than marking the first draft of an essay with a notation for every conceivable error, consider focusing on a single dimension of writing, such as organization, punctuation, or capitalization. By slowing down and taking your time, you send the message that you appreciate each gain your child achieves and that you understand writing to be a process rather than event.

RELISH INVENTION

This book is not an exhaustive treatise on writing, and even if it were, your child would doubtless think of a new method of expression, an alternative graphic organizer, a clever way to combine different writing genres, or a superior way to redraft a scoring rubric. Despite the amount of prescription that appears in many standards documents from state departments of education or local school systems, there is room for creativity, invention, and wonder. If a year from now your child announces that you didn't need that *Reason to Write* book because she has created her own manual for writers, I will be delighted and you should be as well. The key is to move the act of writing from the response to an assignment crafted by an adult to an invention designed by your child.

UNDERSTAND THE GAPS BETWEEN THE OFFICIAL CURRICULUM AND THE "BACKPACK" CURRICULUM

I travel to many schools each year, and when I want to learn about the expectations of teachers in the classroom, I find the official standards document far less illuminating than a review of student work in the classroom. In particular, I focus on the student work that the teacher regards as proficient. In a large number of cases, student writing receives adulation from the teacher and high marks on the report card, but a close examination of the actual student writing reveals that it does not meet the state standards. Thus it is not unusual to find, as I have in a number of districts, that more than half the students who receive nonproficient scores on state tests received passing grades in class. The parents never had a clue that there was something wrong until the state test scores came in. Although there is an impulse to disparage the test and demean the standards, my inquiries usually find that the reason for the disparity between classroom grades and test scores is clear. Classroom grades represent a combination of many things, including attitude, attendance, and effort. Performance on state writing exams, however, represents only proficiency. In the vast majority of schools at every level but particularly at the elementary level, student proficiency is only one of many factors considered in the grades. The other reason for the difference between student test scores and the feedback from the teacher is that the real curriculum—the "backpack curriculum"—does not match state test expectations. Students write stories and personal narratives with splendid results, but the state asks for an analysis of a nonfiction paragraph. Students are directed to give encouraging feedback to other students, but the state requires that they identify errors in sentences. Students receive a single letter grade on an assignment, but the state evaluates student writing using a scoring guide that separately analyzes the mechanics of grammar, spelling, and punctuation, as well as the qualities of organization, sentence transitions, and voice. In sum, parents must know what is actually taught about writing in the classroom, and the only way to understand that is to look with care at the actual work students are expected to complete.

FOCUS YOUR ENERGIES ON "FILLING THE GAPS"

Your child needs a complete set of writing skills. Teachers are frequently too busy with other curriculum demands or the requirements of other curriculum areas to adequately teach and evaluate every type of writing. Moreover, even when teachers attempt to complete a research paper, analyze literature, compare and contrast in social studies, and teach persuasive writing, the effort to cover everything leaves your child with exposure to many things and proficiency at few of the necessary skills. The need for parents to fill in the gaps between the essential curriculum and the actual curriculum is not a criticism of teachers, but recognition of the reality of the classroom. Your attention to these matters may not be greeted with universal enthusiasm by others. For example, you should prepare to endure a few taunts about "hyperactive parents" if you ask your child to write a research paper that is not required in class. Before succumbing to the conventional wisdom that this is just really too, too much for a fifth-grade student, consider two facts. First, virtually every state academic standard requires upper-elementary students to complete a research paper. Second, every state academic standard for middle school students requires a research paper.

The decision you must weigh is whether the criticism you endure for giving your child an enriching writing experience now will be less than the anxiety and stress your child will endure if his first research paper in middle school is a new experience. When you give your child the academic enrichment offered in these pages, you are providing more than an intellectual skill; you are attending to your child's emotional health, reducing future anxiety by perfecting today some essential skills.

EMPOWER YOUR CHILD WITH CHOICE

This book is a menu from which to make choices, not a mountain that you must ascend with dogged persistence. Vary the activities; let your child choose among types of writing, among subjects for exploration, and among the roles of writer, editor, and illustrator. The most important choice that you offer is how to improve thinking, reasoning, and communication. By focusing on the "how" question rather than whether such improvement is a good idea, you empower your child at the same time you place appropriate boundaries around the available choices.

It is not easy to be a parent in the best of times. It is particularly challenging to help children find joy and possibility, and they need not look far to find despair and danger. Despite our best efforts to be protective, our children can be exposed to chilling fear as a result of an errant flip of the television remote control, a casual conversation on the playground, or a simple assignment to listen to the evening news or read the morning paper. A commitment to the writing life will not spare our children from fear, but it will give them the opportunity to express those fears, reflect on them, and think about them with the safe and loving guidance of a parent. The reason to write analytically and persuasively is ultimately not the fulfillment of an assignment in school, but the need for thinking through the challenges that our children and our world must face. The reason to write creatively and with passion is the need for describing a world in which our children see beauty and potential that can frequently elude their preoccupied parents. The young authors in your home will never have a more patient, interested, or important reader than you.

Appendix A

California Academic Content Standards—Writing: Grades 1–5

Grade 1
Writing

1.0 Writing Strategies
Students write clear and coherent sentences and paragraphs that develop a central idea. Their writing shows they consider the audience and purpose. Students progress through the stages of the writing process (e.g., prewriting, drafting, revising, editing successive versions).

ORGANIZATION AND FOCUS
   1.1 Select a focus when writing.
   1.2 Use descriptive words when writing.

PENMANSHIP
   1.3 Print legibly and space letters, words, and sentences appropriately.

2.0 Writing Applications (Genres and Their Characteristics)
Students write compositions that describe and explain familiar objects, events, and experiences. Student writing demonstrates a command of standard American English and the drafting, research, and organizational strategies outlined in Writing Standard 1.0.

   Using the writing strategies of grade one outlined in Writing Standard 1.0, students:
   2.1 Write brief narratives (e.g., fictional, autobiographical) describing an experience.
   2.2 Write brief expository descriptions of a real object, person, place, or event, using sensory details.

Written and Oral English Language Conventions

The standards for written and oral English language conventions have been placed between those for writing and for listening and speaking because these conventions are essential to both sets of skills.

1.0 Written and Oral English Language Conventions
Students write and speak with a command of standard English conventions appropriate to this grade level.

SENTENCE STRUCTURE
1.1 Write and speak in complete, coherent sentences.

GRAMMAR
1.2 Identify and correctly use singular and plural nouns.

1.3 Identify and correctly use contractions (e.g., *isn't, aren't, can't, won't*) and singular possessive pronouns (e.g., *my/mine, his/her, hers, your/s*) in writing and speaking.

PUNCTUATION
1.4 Distinguish between declarative, exclamatory, and interrogative sentences.

1.5 Use a period, exclamation point, or question mark at the end of sentences.

1.6 Use knowledge of the basic rules of punctuation and capitalization when writing.

CAPITALIZATION
1.7 Capitalize the first word of a sentence, names of people, and the pronoun I.

SPELLING
1.8 Spell three-and four-letter short-vowel words and grade-level-appropriate sight words correctly.

Grade 2
Writing

1.0 Writing Strategies
Students write clear and coherent sentences and paragraphs that develop a central idea. Their writing shows they consider the audience and purpose. Students progress through the stages of the writing process (e.g., prewriting, drafting, revising, editing successive versions).

ORGANIZATION AND FOCUS
1.1 Group related ideas and maintain a consistent focus.

PENMANSHIP
1.2 Create readable documents with legible handwriting.

RESEARCH

1.3 Understand the purposes of various reference materials (e.g., dictionary, thesaurus, atlas).

EVALUATION AND REVISION

1.4 Revise original drafts to improve sequence and provide more descriptive detail.

2.0 Writing Applications (Genres and Their Characteristics)

Students write compositions that describe and explain familiar objects, events, and experiences. Student writing demonstrates a command of standard American English and the drafting, research, and organizational strategies outlined in Writing Standard 1.0.

Using the writing strategies of grade two outlined in Writing Standard 1.0, students:

2.1 Write brief narratives based on their experiences:

a. Move through a logical sequence of events.

b. Describe the setting, characters, objects, and events in detail.

2.2 Write a friendly letter complete with the date, salutation, body, closing, and signature.

Written and Oral English Language Conventions

The standards for written and oral English language conventions have been placed between those for writing and for listening and speaking because these conventions are essential to both sets of skills.

1.0 Written and Oral English Language Conventions

Students write and speak with a command of standard English conventions appropriate to this grade level.

SENTENCE STRUCTURE

1.1 Distinguish between complete and incomplete sentences.

1.2 Recognize and use the correct word order in written sentences.

GRAMMAR

1.3 Identify and correctly use various parts of speech, including nouns and verbs, in writing and speaking.

PUNCTUATION

1.4 Use commas in the greeting and closure of a letter and with dates and items in a series.

1.5 Use quotation marks correctly.

CAPITALIZATION

1.6 Capitalize all proper nouns, words at the beginning of sentences and greetings, months and days of the week, and titles and initials of people.

SPELLING

1.7 Spell frequently used, irregular words correctly (e.g., *was, were, says, said, who, what, why*).

1.8 Spell basic short-vowel, long-vowel, r-controlled, and consonant-blend patterns correctly.

Grade 3
Writing

1.0 Writing Strategies

Students write clear and coherent sentences and paragraphs that develop a central idea. Their writing shows they consider the audience and purpose. Students progress through the stages of the writing process (e.g., prewriting, drafting, revising, editing successive versions).

ORGANIZATION AND FOCUS

1.1 Create a single paragraph:

a. Develop a topic sentence.

b. Include simple supporting facts and details.

PENMANSHIP

1.2 Write legibly in cursive or joined italic, allowing margins and correct spacing between letters in a word and words in a sentence.

RESEARCH

1.3 Understand the structure and organization of various reference materials (e.g., dictionary, thesaurus, atlas, encyclopedia).

EVALUATION AND REVISION

1.4 Revise drafts to improve the coherence and logical progression of ideas by using an established rubric.

2.0 Writing Applications (Genres and Their Characteristics)

Students write compositions that describe and explain familiar objects, events, and experiences. Student writing demonstrates a command of standard American English and the drafting, research, and organizational strategies outlined in Writing Standard 1.0.

Using the writing strategies of grade three outlined in Writing Standard 1.0, students:

2.1 Write narratives:

a. Provide a context within which an action takes place.

b. Include well-chosen details to develop the plot.

c. Provide insight into why the selected incident is memorable.

2.2 Write descriptions that use concrete sensory details to present and support unified impressions of people, places, things, or experiences.

2.3 Write personal and formal letters, thank-you notes, and invitations:
a. Show awareness of the knowledge and interests of the audience and establish a purpose and context.
b. Include the date, proper salutation, body, closing, and signature.

Written and Oral English Language Conventions

The standards for written and oral English language conventions have been placed between those for writing and for listening and speaking because these conventions are essential to both sets of skills.

1.0 Written and Oral English Language Conventions
Students write and speak with a command of standard English conventions appropriate to this grade level.

SENTENCE STRUCTURE
1.1 Understand and be able to use complete and correct declarative, interrogative, imperative, and exclamatory sentences in writing and speaking.

GRAMMAR
1.2 Identify subjects and verbs that are in agreement and identify and use pronouns, adjectives, compound words, and articles correctly in writing and speaking.
1.3 Identify and use past, present, and future verb tenses properly in writing and speaking.
1.4 Identify and use subjects and verbs correctly in speaking and writing simple sentences.

PUNCTUATION
1.5 Punctuate dates, city and state, and titles of books correctly.
1.6 Use commas in dates, locations, and addresses and for items in a series.

CAPITALIZATION
1.7 Capitalize geographical names, holidays, historical periods, and special events correctly.

SPELLING
1.8 Spell correctly one-syllable words that have blends, contractions, compounds, orthographic patterns (e.g., qu, consonant doubling, changing the ending of a word from -y to -ies when forming the plural), and common homophones (e.g., hair-hare). 1.9 Arrange words in alphabetic order.

Grade 4
Writing

1.0 Writing Strategies

Students write clear, coherent sentences and paragraphs that develop a central idea. Their writing shows they consider the audience and purpose. Students progress through the stages of the writing process (e.g., prewriting, drafting, revising, editing successive versions).

ORGANIZATION AND FOCUS

1.1 Select a focus, an organizational structure, and a point of view based upon purpose, audience, length, and format requirements.

1.2 Create multiple-paragraph compositions:

a. Provide an introductory paragraph.

b. Establish and support a central idea with a topic sentence at or near the beginning of the first paragraph.

c. Include supporting paragraphs with simple facts, details, and explanations.

d. Conclude with a paragraph that summarizes the points.

e. Use correct indention.

1.3 Use traditional structures for conveying information (e.g., chronological order, cause and effect, similarity and difference, and posing and answering a question).

PENMANSHIP

1.4 Write fluidly and legibly in cursive or joined italic.

RESEARCH AND TECHNOLOGY

1.5 Quote or paraphrase information sources, citing them appropriately.

1.6 Locate information in reference texts by using organizational features (e.g., prefaces, appendixes).

1.7 Use various reference materials (e.g., dictionary, thesaurus, card catalog, encyclopedia, online information) as an aid to writing.

1.8 Understand the organization of almanacs, newspapers, and periodicals and how to use those print materials.

1.9 Demonstrate basic keyboarding skills and familiarity with computer terminology (e.g., cursor, software, memory, disk drive, hard drive).

EVALUATION AND REVISION

1.10 Edit and revise selected drafts to improve coherence and progression by adding, deleting, consolidating, and rearranging text.

2.0 Writing Applications (Genres and Their Characteristics)

Students write compositions that describe and explain familiar objects, events, and experiences. Student writing demonstrates a command of standard American English and the drafting, research, and organizational strategies outlined in Writing Standard 1.0.

Using the writing strategies of grade four outlined in Writing Standard 1.0, students:

2.1 Write narratives:

a. Relate ideas, observations, or recollections of an event or experience.

b. Provide a context to enable the reader to imagine the world of the event or experience.

c. Use concrete sensory details.

d. Provide insight into why the selected event or experience is memorable.

2.2 Write responses to literature:

a. Demonstrate an understanding of the literary work.

b. Support judgments through references to both the text and prior knowledge.

2.3 Write information reports:

a. Frame a central question about an issue or situation.

b. Include facts and details for focus.

c. Draw from more than one source of information (e.g., speakers, books, newspapers, other media sources).

2.4 Write summaries that contain the main ideas of the reading selection and the most significant details.

Written and Oral English Language Conventions

The standards for written and oral English language conventions have been placed between those for writing and for listening and speaking because these conventions are essential to both sets of skills.

1.0 Written and Oral English Language Conventions
Students write and speak with a command of standard English conventions appropriate to this grade level.

SENTENCE STRUCTURE
1.1 Use simple and compound sentences in writing and speaking.

1.2 Combine short, related sentences with appositives, participial phrases, adjectives, ad-verbs, and prepositional phrases.

GRAMMAR
1.3 Identify and use regular and irregular verbs, adverbs, prepositions, and coordinating conjunctions in writing and speaking.

PUNCTUATION
1.4 Use parentheses, commas in direct quotations, and apostrophes in the possessive case of nouns and in contractions.

1.5 Use underlining, quotation marks, or italics to identify titles of documents.

CAPITALIZATION

1.6 Capitalize names of magazines, newspapers, works of art, musical compositions, organizations, and the first word in quotations when appropriate.

SPELLING

1.7 Spell correctly roots, inflections, suffixes and prefixes, and syllable constructions.

Grade 5
Writing

1.0 Writing Strategies

Students write clear, coherent, and focused essays. The writing exhibits the students' awareness of the audience and purpose. Essays contain formal introductions, supporting evidence, and conclusions. Students progress through the stages of the writing process as needed.

ORGANIZATION AND FOCUS

1.1 Create multiple-paragraph narrative compositions:

a. Establish and develop a situation or plot.

b. Describe the setting.

c. Present an ending.

1.2 Create multiple-paragraph expository compositions:

a. Establish a topic, important ideas, or events in sequence or chronological order.

b. Provide details and transitional expressions that link one paragraph to another in a clear line of thought.

c. Offer a concluding paragraph that summarizes important ideas and details.

RESEARCH AND TECHNOLOGY

1.3 Use organizational features of printed text (e.g., citations, end notes, bibliographic references) to locate relevant information.

1.4 Create simple documents by using electronic media and employing organizational features (e.g., passwords, entry and pull-down menus, word searches, the thesaurus, spell checks).

1.5 Use a thesaurus to identify alternative word choices and meanings.

EVALUATION AND REVISION

1.6 Edit and revise manuscripts to improve the meaning and focus of writing by adding, deleting, consolidating, clarifying, and rearranging words and sentences.

2.0 Writing Applications (Genres and Their Characteristics)

Students write narrative, expository, persuasive, and descriptive texts of at least 500 to 700 words in each genre. Student writing demonstrates a command of standard American English and the research, organizational, and drafting strategies outlined in Writing Standard 1.0.

Using the writing strategies of grade five outlined in Writing Standard 1.0, students:

2.1 Write narratives:
a. Establish a plot, point of view, setting, and conflict.
b. Show, rather than tell, the events of the story.

2.2 Write responses to literature:
a. Demonstrate an understanding of a literary work.
b. Support judgments through references to the text and to prior knowledge.
c. Develop interpretations that exhibit careful reading and understanding.

2.3 Write research reports about important ideas, issues, or events by using the following guidelines:
a. Frame questions that direct the investigation.
b. Establish a controlling idea or topic.
c. Develop the topic with simple facts, details, examples, and explanations.

2.4 Write persuasive letters or compositions:
a. State a clear position in support of a proposal.
b. Support a position with relevant evidence.
c. Follow a simple organizational pattern.
d. Address reader concerns.

Written and Oral English Language Conventions

The standards for written and oral English language conventions have been placed between those for writing and for listening and speaking because these conventions are essential to both sets of skills.

1.0 Written and Oral English Language Conventions

Students write and speak with a command of standard English conventions appropriate to this grade level.

SENTENCE STRUCTURE
1.1 Identify and correctly use prepositional phrases, appositives, and independent and dependent clauses; use transitions and conjunctions to connect ideas.

GRAMMAR

1.2 Identify and correctly use verbs that are often misused (e.g., lie/ lay, sit/ set, rise/ raise), modifiers, and pronouns.

PUNCTUATION

1.3 Use a colon to separate hours and minutes and to introduce a list; use quotation marks around the exact words of a speaker and titles of poems, songs, short stories, and so forth.

CAPITALIZATION

1.4. Use correct capitalization.

SPELLING

1.5 Spell roots, suffixes, prefixes, contractions, and syllable constructions correctly.

Internet Links to State Standards

Alabama: http://www.alsde.edu/ver1/section_detail.asp?section=54

Alaska: http://www.eed.state.ak.us/qschools/standards.html

Arizona: http://www.ade.state.az.us/standards/contentstandards.htm

Arkansas: http://arkedu.state.ar.us/standard.htm

California: http://goldmine.cde.ca.gov/board/

Colorado: http://www.cde.state.co.us/index_stnd.htm

Connecticut: http://www.state.ct.us/sde/dtl/curriculum/index.htm

Delaware: http://www.doe.state.de.us/DPIServices/Desk_Ref/DOE_DeskRef.htm#This

Florida: http://www.firn.edu/doe/curric/prek12/frame2.htm

Georgia: http://www.glc.k12.ga.us/qstd-int/homepg.htm

Hawaii: http://165.248.10.190/HCPS/L2/hcps6.nsf/

Idaho: http://www.sde.state.id.us/osbe/exstand.htm

Illinois: http://www.isbe.state.il.us/ils/

Indiana: http://doe.state.in.us/standards/welcome.html

Iowa: http://www.state.ia.us/educate/index.html

Kansas: http://www.ksbe.state.ks.us/Welcome.html

Kentucky: http://www.kde.state.ky.us/oapd/curric/Publications/Transformations/vol1into.html

Louisiana: http://www.doe.state.la.us/DOE/asps/home.asp?I=HOME

Maine: http://janus.state.me.us/education/g2000/linktool.htm

Maryland: http://www.mdk12.org/mspp/standards/index.html

Massachusetts: http://www.doe.mass.edu/frameworks/current.html

Michigan: http://cdp.mde.state.mi.us/MCF/default.html

Minnesota: http://cfl.state.mn.us/GRAD/gradhom.htm

Mississippi: http://www.mde.k12.ms.us/curriculum/

Missouri: http://www.dese.state.mo.us/standards/

Montana: http://www.metnet.state.mt.us/Montana%20Education/OPI/School%20Improvement/HTM/Mt-standards.shtml

Nebraska: http://www.nde.state.ne.us/Issu/AcadStand.html

Nevada: http://www.nde.state.ne.us/Issu/AcadStand.html

New Hampshire: http://www.ed.state.nh.us/CurriculumFrameworks/curricul.htm

New Jersey: http://www.state.nj.us/njded/cccs/index.html

New Mexico: http://sde.state.nm.us/divisions/learningservices/schoolprogram/standards/csnb.html

New York: http://www.emsc.nysed.gov/ciai/pub.html

North Carolina: http://www.dpi.state.nc.us/curriculum/

North Dakota: http://www.dpi.state.nd.us/standard/content.shtm

Ohio: http://www.ode.state.oh.us/ca/ci/

Oklahoma: http://sde.state.ok.us/publ/pass.html

Oregon: http://www.ode.state.or.us/TchgLrngStds/intro.htm

Pennsylvania: http://www.pde.psu.edu/regs/chapter4.html

Rhode Island: http://www.ridoe.net/standards/frameworks/default.htm

South Carolina: http://www.state.sc.us/sde/test123/standard.htm

South Dakota: http://www.state.sd.us/deca/ContentStandards/index.htm

Tennessee: http://www.state.tn.us/education/ci/cicurframwkmain.htm

Texas: http://www.tea.state.tx.us/teks/

Utah: http://www.uen.org/cgi-bin/websql/utahlink/CoreHome.hts

Vermont: http://www.state.vt.us/educ/stand/framework.htm

Virginia: http://www.knowledge.state.va.us/main/sol/sol.cfm

Washington: http://www.k12.wa.us/reform/EALR/default.asp

West Virginia: http://wvde.state.wv.us/igos/

Wisconsin: http://www.dpi.state.wi.us/standards/index.html

Wyoming: http://www.k12.wy.us/publications/standards.html

Appendix B

Scoring Rubrics for State Writing Tests

The following four-point holistic rubric will be used to score the Grade 4 Writing Standards Test. The rubric includes general criteria related to writing strategies and conventions, as well as specific criteria for each writing genre included in the Writing Applications standards.

Grade-4 students may be asked to write a narrative, a response to literature, or a summary. Information on specific writing expectations, Curricular and Instructional Profiles, and assessment strategies for teachers to use in monitoring student progress are included in the *Reading/Language Arts Framework for California Public Schools, Kindergarten Through Grade Twelve*. The framework may be accessed at http://www.cde.ca.gov/cdepress/lang_arts.pdf.

California
Scoring Rubric for Grade 4 California Writing Standards Tests

4

The Writing
- clearly addresses all parts of the writing task
- demonstrates a clear understanding of purpose
- maintains a consistent point of view, focus, and organizational structure, including paragraphing when appropriate
- includes a clearly presented central idea with relevant facts, details, and/or explanations
- includes a variety of sentence types
- contains few, if any, errors in the conventions of the English language (grammar, punctuation, capitalization, spelling). These errors do not interfere with the reader's understanding of the writing.

Narrative
- provides a thoroughly developed sequence of significant events to relate ideas, observations, and/or memories
- includes vivid descriptive language and sensory details that enable the reader to visualize the events or experiences

Summary
- is characterized by paraphrasing of the main idea(s) and significant details

Response to Literature
- demonstrates a clear understanding of the literary work
- provides effective support for judgments through specific references to text and prior knowledge

3

The Writing
- addresses all parts of the writing task
- demonstrates a general understanding of purpose
- maintains a mostly consistent point of view, focus, and organizational structure, including paragraphing when appropriate
- presents a central idea with mostly relevant facts, details, and/or explanations
- includes a variety of sentence types
- contains some errors in the conventions of the English language (grammar, punctuation, capitalization, spelling). These errors do not interfere with the reader's understanding of the writing.

Narrative
- provides an adequately developed sequence of significant events to relate ideas, observations, and/or memories
- includes some descriptive language and sensory details that enable the reader to visualize the events or experiences

Summary
- is characterized by paraphrasing of the main idea(s) and significant details

Response to Literature
- demonstrates an understanding of the literary work
- provides some support for judgments through references to text and prior knowledge

2

The Writing
- addresses only parts of the writing task
- demonstrates little understanding of purpose
- maintains an inconsistent point of view, focus, and/or organizational structure
- suggests a central idea with limited facts, details, and/or explanations
- includes little variety in sentence types
- contains several errors in the conventions of the English language (grammar, punctuation, capitalization, spelling). These errors may interfere with the reader's understanding of the writing.

Narrative
- provides a minimally developed sequence of events to relate ideas, observations, and/or memories
- includes limited descriptive language and sensory details that enable the reader to visualize the events or experiences

Summary
- is characterized by substantial copying of key phrases and minimal paraphrasing

Response to Literature
- demonstrates a limited understanding of the literary work
- provides weak support for judgments

1 The Writing

- addresses only one part of the writing task
- demonstrates no understanding of purpose
- lacks a clear point of view, focus, and/or organizational structure
- lacks a central idea but may contain marginally related facts, details, and/or explanations
- includes no sentence variety
- contains serious errors in the conventions of the English language (grammar, punctuation, capitalization, spelling). These errors interfere with the reader's understanding of the writing.

Narrative

- lacks a sequence of events to relate ideas, observations, and/or memories
- lacks descriptive language and sensory details that enable the reader to visualize the events or experiences

Summary

- is characterized by substantial copying of indiscriminately selected phrases or sentences

Response to Literature

- demonstrates little understanding of the literary work
- fails to provide support for judgments

Colorado
Colorado "Kid-friendly" Writing Rubric

4 Points: My writing is clear and does what the prompt asked me. My errors in spelling and punctuation are so few they wouldn't bother you.

CONTENT AND ORGANIZATION

☑ I used important details and information.

☑ I did not forget or lose the main idea when I added interesting details.

☑ I was careful to organize the ideas logically and effectively.

☑ I made sure all of my details connect to the prompt.

STYLE

☑ My word choice is awesome. The words fit the prompt well.

☑ I tried to use interesting words or descriptions to make pictures in the reader's mind.

☑ My sentences are not all the same. I used different sentences.

☑ My writing is neat and almost perfect.

3 Points: My writing is pretty good. I did what the prompt asked of me, but I did not give enough information or details with my answer. I need to add more. I made very few errors in spelling and punctuation.

CONTENT AND ORGANIZATION

☑ I explained my main idea, but I need to add more information. I need to choose more important details and take out those that aren't.

☑ Sometimes my writing moves away from the main point or details get in the way of the main point.

☑ I need to put my story in order.

☑ I need to connect ideas so that they all fit well together.

STYLE

☑ Most of my words go well with the purpose.

☑ At times I could have chosen better words.

☑ My sentences are well written, but I did not try different kinds of sentences.

☑ Most of my paper is neat and easy to read.

☑ I may have made a mistake in grammar, spelling, or punctuation, but you can still understand what I mean.

Colorado
Colorado "Kid-friendly" Writing Rubric

2 Points: My writing is not clear enough, and I drifted away from the prompt. I need to use more details and be sure they are accurate. I did not notice the errors I made in spelling and mechanics.

CONTENT AND ORGANIZATION

- ☑ I need to write more clearly and be sure I keep the purpose in mind. I need to be sure I have told all that I can to make my paper complete.

- ☑ I may not have included enough details, or I may have spent too much time on the details and forgot the purpose.

- ☑ My writing may seem more like a list than like a paragraph with ideas that go together.

- ☑ I need to be sure my writing stays on topic.

STYLE

- ☑ I need to use words that are strong and effective.

- ☑ My writing is not smooth, and I repeat myself at times.

- ☑ Sometimes you can't read my writing, and I need to be more careful about spelling and mechanics.

1 Point: My writing needs to be focused and organized. I need to write more to the prompt and include a lot more details and information. I have too many mistakes in spelling and mechanics.

CONTENT AND ORGANIZATION

- ☑ I have not paid enough attention to what I am supposed to write.

- ☑ I need to include a lot more information.

- ☑ I need to organize my ideas so that my writing is clear.

- ☑ I need to make sure my writing is complete and about the topic.

STYLE

- ☑ I need to write so that others can read it.

- ☑ I need to choose a variety of words and be sure that they are just right.

- ☑ I need to learn more words.

- ☑ I need to write complete sentences.

- ☑ My mistakes in spelling and mechanics keep my reader from understanding what I meant.

Florida Writing Assessment Program
FCAT Writing Rubric

The rubric interprets the four major areas of consideration into levels of achievement.

6 Points

The writing is focused, purposeful, and reflects insight into the writing situation. The paper conveys a sense of completeness and wholeness with adherence to the main idea, and its organizational pattern provides for a logical progression of ideas. The support is substantial, specific, relevant, concrete, and/or illustrative. The paper demonstrates a commitment to and an involvement with the subject, clarity in presentation of ideas, and may use creative writing strategies appropriate to the purpose of the paper. The writing demonstrates a mature command of language (word choice) with freshness of expression. Sentence structure is varied, and sentences are complete except when fragments are used purposefully. Few, if any, convention errors occur in mechanics, usage, and punctuation.

5 Points

The writing focuses on the topic, and its organizational pattern provides for a progression of ideas, although some lapses may occur. The paper conveys a sense of completeness or wholeness. The support is ample. The writing demonstrates a mature command of language, including precision in word choice. There is variation in sentence structure, and, with rare exceptions, sentences are complete except when fragments are used purposefully. The paper generally follows the conventions of mechanics, usage, and spelling.

4 Points

The writing is generally focused on the topic but may include extraneous or loosely related material. An organizational pattern is apparent, although some lapses may occur. The paper exhibits some sense of completeness or wholeness. The support, including word choice, is adequate, although development may be uneven. There is little variation in sentence structure, and most sentences are complete. The paper generally follows the conventions of mechanics, usage, and spelling.

3 Points

The writing is generally focused on the topic but may include extraneous or loosely related material. An organizational pattern has been attempted, but the paper may lack a sense of completeness or wholeness. Some support is included, but development is erratic. Word choice is adequate but may be limited, predictable, or occasionally vague. There is little, if any, variation in sentence structure. Knowledge of the conventions of mechanics and usage is usually demonstrated, and commonly used words are usually spelled correctly.

2 Points

The writing is related to the topic but may include extraneous or loosely related material. Little evidence of an organizational pattern may be demonstrated, and the paper may lack a sense of completeness or wholeness. Development of support is inadequate or illogical. Word choice is limited, inappropriate or vague. There is little, if any, variation in sentence structure, and gross errors in sentence structure may occur. Errors in basic conventions of mechanics and usage may occur, and commonly used words may be misspelled.

1 Point

The writing may only minimally address the topic. The paper is a fragmentary or incoherent listing of related ideas or sentences or both. Little, if any, development of support or an organizational pattern or both is apparent. Limited or inappropriate word choice may obscure meaning. Gross errors in sentence structure and usage may impede communication. Frequent and blatant errors may occur in the basic conventions of mechanics and usage, and commonly used words may be misspelled.

Unscorable

The paper is unscorable because:

- the response is not related to what the prompt requested the student to do.
- the response is simply a rewording of the prompt.
- the response is a copy of a published work.
- the student refused to write.
- the response is illegible.
- the response is incomprehensible (words are arranged in such a way that no meaning is conveyed).
- the response contains an insufficient amount of writing to determine if the student was attempting to address the prompt.
- the writing folder is blank.

North Carolina
The Narrative Composition Focused Holistic Score Scale
Fourth Grade Writing Assessment Rubric

Score Point 4

The response exhibits a strong command of narrative writing. The response is focused and has an effective sequencing of events and a clear progression of ideas. The writer provides specific, relevant details to support ideas. The composition is unified and well elaborated. The writer's organization provides a clear strategy or controlled plan; the composition progresses logically and has a sense of overall completeness.

Score Point 3

The response exhibits a reasonable command of narrative writing. The response is focused and establishes progression of ideas and events although minor lapses in focus and progression may be present. The composition contains elaboration and support in the form of specific details. The composition may have minor weaknesses in coherence. The writer's organization provides a reasonable sense of logical progression and overall completeness.

Score Point 2

The response exhibits a weak command of narrative writing. The response exhibits some progression of ideas and events and provides some elaboration and support. The elaboration is relevant but may be flawed. The composition may not be evenly elaborated, having a list-like quality with concrete supporting details. The composition may have little connection between a controlling idea and supporting details relevant to development.

Score Point 1

The response exhibits a lack of command of narrative writing. There is evidence that the writer has read the prompt and attempted to respond to it. The writer may attempt to support ideas, but there may be no sense of strategy or control, or the writer may exhibit skeletal control but the response is too sparse to be scored higher than a "1." The response may not sustain focus on the topic, may lack clarity, and /or may have an inappropriate strategy.

NS This code may be used for compositions that are entirely illegible or otherwise unscorable: blank responses, responses written in a foreign language, restatements of the prompt, and responses that are off topic or incoherent. The Scoring Director must give permission for the use of "NS."

Texas

Grade 4 Writing Rubric
SCORING TAAS COMPOSITIONS

A process called focused holistic scoring is used to evaluate each TAAS written composition. This scoring system is "holistic" because the piece of writing is considered as a whole. It is "focused in that the piece of writing is evaluated according to pre established criteria. These criteria, which take into account the student's developmental capabilities and constraints of the testing situation, correspond to the first four objectives listed in the *Educators Guide to the TEKS-Based Assessment.*

> Objective 1: The student will respond appropriately in a written composition to the purpose/audience specified in a given topic.
> Objective 2: The student will organize idea in a written composition on a given topic.
> Objective 3: The student will demonstrate control of the English Language in a written composition on a given topic.
> Objective 4: The student will generate a written composition that develops/supports/elaborates the central idea stated in a given topic.

Each TAAS response is evaluated according to the extent to which it reflects mastery of these four objectives. The response is scored on a scale of 1 (low) to 4 (high). A student may also receive a rating of 0, indicating that the response could not be scored. Nonscorable responses include those that are off-topic, those that are indecipherable, and those that are insufficient responses to the specified task.

SCORE POINT 1

1 = RESPONSES THAT ATTEMPT TO TELL A STORY BUT ARE NOT SUCCESSFUL. THE FOLLOWING TYPES OF RESPONSES FALL INTO THE "1" CATEGORY:

Responses that use the wrong purpose; i.e., they do not link a sequence of events through time. In some of these responses, the writer may briefly tell a story. In other responses the writer tells no story at all. In both cases, it appears that the intent of the writer is to focus on a purpose for writer other than the one specified in the prompt.

Responses that are unsuccessful attempts to tell a story. These responses may take the following forms:

· *Responses that contain a brief phrase indicating that the student has attempted to tell a story.*

· *Responses that contain a sequence of events, but the sequence is not sustained sufficiently to be minimally successful.*

· Responses that contain major gaps that make the story line confusing and difficult to follow.

· Responses that attend to the task but then drift from the specified topic.

· Responses that attend to the task but then drift from the specified purpose.

Responses that lack clarity.

· These responses may contain incomplete or illogical thought, making the meaning unclear.

· These responses may lack even implicit connections between ideas, causing confusion.

Responses that exhibit an overall lack of control of written language so that communication is impaired. In each of these responses, the expression of the writer's thoughts is so confusing that the reader is left wondering what the writer was attempting to say. Errors in spelling, capitalization, punctuation, and usage are considered language control problems if they are so frequent or severe that they interfere with the reader's ability to understand the response.

In addition, these responses may be poorly organized. The writer may present events in a random or repetitive fashion.

SCORE POINT 2

2 = RESPONSES THAT ARE MINIMALLY SUCCESSFUL ATTEMPTS TO TELL A STORY.

The following types of responses fall into the "2" category:

· Responses that contain a barely controlled sequence of events.

· Responses that contain a somewhat elaborated sequence of events, although gaps and/or digressions may occur.

These responses may be characterized by any of the following:

· A substantial amount of nonnarrative writing.

· One or more organizational strategies that are flawed. In these responses narrative clusters may be evident, but the story line may be interrupted by randomness or repetition.

· A limited control of written language. These responses may contain awkward or simplistic sentence structures and word choice may be limited. Some errors in spelling, capitalization, punctuation, and/or usage may occur, although these errors do not cause confusion.

SCORE POINT 3

3 = RESPONSES THAT REPRESENT GOOD ATTEMPTS TO TELL A STORY. THE READER HAS NO DIFFICULTY FOLLOWING THE STORY LINE.

These responses contain a moderately elaborated sequence of events. The elaboration adds substance to the story line, although there may be occasional gaps and/or digressions.

These responses may be characterized by the following:

- *One or more organizational strategies that are, for the most part, consistent, although occasional inconsistencies may occur.*

- *A general control of written language, although some errors in spelling, capitalization, punctuation, and/or usage may occur, since these responses do not represent "polished" pieces of writing.*

SCORE POINT 4

4 = RESPONSES THAT ARE CONSISTENT, ORGANIZED, AND ELABORATED STORIES. THESE RESPONSES ARE UNIFIED AND EASY TO READ. THE INCONSISTENCIES THAT MAY OCCUR ARE OVERWHELMED BY THE OVERALL QUALITY OF THE RESPONSES.

These responses contain a controlled, well-elaborated sequence of events. The responses follow the narrative progression from beginning to end. The writers do not make abrupt shifts in time or location. When shifts in time or location occur, the writers handle them effectively.

These responses are characterized by most of the following:

- *One or more consistent organizational strategies.* Although minor inconsistencies may occur, the responses have a clear sense of order and completeness. If otherwise well-written stories end abruptly because the writers have run out of space, the responses are still eligible for a 4.

- *A consistent control of written language.* Although the writers may not incorporate all of the appropriate mechanics or conventions of language, the responses are nevertheless effective.

- *Varied syntactic constructions, including compound and complex sentences.*

- *Rich details that embellish the unfolding of events.*

- *Effective word choice, including vivid words, phrases, and expressions.*

Appendix C

State Writing Test Table

STATE	GRADES AT WHICH WRITING IS TESTED	TESTING INSTRUMENT(S)
Alabama	3-8	Stanford 9
Alaska	3,5,8,10	Benchmark Exams HSGQE (High School Graduation Qualifying Exam)
Arizona	3,5,8,10	AIMS (Arizona Instrument to Measure Standards)
Arkansas	4,8, HS	Benchmark Exams EOC (End Of Course)
California	4,7,10	STAR (Standardized Testing And Reporting) CAHSEE (California High School Exit Exam)
Colorado	3-10	CSAP (Colorado Student Assessment Program)
Connecticut	4,6,8	CMT (Connecticut Mastery Test)
Delaware	3,5,8,10	DSTP (Delaware State Testing Program)
District of Columbia	N/A	N/A
Florida	4,8,10	FCAT (Florida Comprehensive Assessment Test)
Georgia	3,5,8,HS	GTWA (Grade Three Writing Assessment) GFWA (Grade Five Writing Assessment) MGWA (Middle Grades Writing Assessment) GHSWT (Georgia High School Writing Test)

STATE	GRADES AT WHICH WRITING IS TESTED	TESTING INSTRUMENT(S)
Hawaii	3,5,8	HCPS II (Hawaii Content And Performance Standards, Second Edition)
Idaho	4,8,10	DWA (Direct Writing Assessment)
Indiana	3,6,8,11	ISTEP+ (Indiana Statewide Testing for Educational Progress-Plus) GQE (Graduation Qualifying Exam)
Illinois	3,5,8,11	ISAT (Illinois Standard Achievement Test) PSAE (Prairie State Achievement Exam)
Iowa	N/A	N/A
Kansas	5,8,11	KAP (Kansas Assessment Program)
Kentucky	4,7,12	KCCT (Kentucky Core Content Test)
Louisiana	4,8,10	LEAP 21, (Louisiana Education Assessment Program for the 21st Century) GEE 21 (Graduation Exit Exam for the 21st Century)
Maine	4,8, 11	MEA (Maine Educational Assessments)
Maryland	3,5,8	MSPAP (Maryland School Performance Assessment Program)

STATE	GRADES AT WHICH WRITING IS TESTED	TESTING INSTRUMENT(S)
Massachusetts	4,7	MCAS (Massachusetts Comprehensive Assessment System)
Michigan	5,7,11 (4,7,11 from 2002-03)	MEAP (Michigan Educational Assessment Program)
Minnesota	5,10	MCA (Minnesota Comprehensive Assessment) BST (Basic Skills Test)
Mississippi	4,7,HS	MCT (Missouri Curriculum Tests) SATP (Subject Area Testing Program) FLE (Functional Literacy Exam)
Missouri	3,7,11	MAP (Missouri Assessment Program)
Montana	8	NAEP (National Assessment of Educational Progress)
Nebraska	4,8,11	SWA (Statewide Writing Assessment)
Nevada	4,8,12	NVWA (Nevada Writing Assessment)
New Hampshire	3,6,10	NHIEAP (New Hampshire Educational Improvement and Assessment Program)
New Jersey	4,8,11	ESPA (Elementary School Proficiency Assessment) GEPA (Grade Eight Performance Assessment) HSPA (High School Proficiency Assessment)

STATE	GRADES AT WHICH WRITING IS TESTED	TESTING INSTRUMENT(S)
New Mexico	5,7,HS	NMWAP (New Mexico Writing Assessment Program) NMHSCE (New Mexico High School Comprehensive Exam)
New York	4,8,HS	NYS Tests, Regents
North Carolina	4,7,HS	NCWA (North Carolina Writing Assessment) NCHSEE (North Carolina High School Exit Exam)
North Dakota	4,8	NDWT (North Dakota Writing Test)
Ohio	4,6	OPT (Ohio Proficiency Tests)
Oklahoma	5,8,10	OCCT (Oklahoma Core Curriculum Test)
Oregon	5,8	Benchmark Tests/CIM (Certificate of Initial Mastery Tests)
Pennsylvania	6,9,11	PSSA (Pennsylvania System for Student Assessment)
Rhode Island	3,7,10	RIWA (Rhode Island Writing Assessment)
South Carolina	3-8	PACT (Palmetto Achievement Challenge Test)
South Dakota	5,9	SWA (Stanford Writing Assessment)
Tennessee	4,7,10	TCAP-WA (Tennessee Comprehensive Assessment Program-Writing Assessment)

STATE	GRADES AT WHICH WRITING IS TESTED	TESTING INSTRUMENT(S)
Texas	4,8,10 (4,7,11 from 2003 with TAKS)	TAAS (Texas Assessment of Academic Skills) TAKS (Texas Assessment of Knowledge and Skills)
Utah	6,9	UTWA (Utah Writing Assessment)
Vermont	4,8,10	VTWA (Vermont Writing Assessment)
Virginia	5,8,11	SOL (Standards of Learning)
Washington	4,7,10	WASL (Washington Assessment of Student Learning)
West Virginia	4,7,10	WVWA (West Virginia Writing Assessment)
Wisconsin	4,8,10	WKCE (Wisconsin Knowledge and Concepts Examinations)
Wyoming	4,8,11	WyCAS (Wyoming Comprehensive Assessment System)

Appendix D

SELECTED RESOURCES FOR PARENTS AND TEACHERS

TEACHING YOUNG WRITERS

Calkins, Lucy McCormick. *The Art of Teaching Writing,* 2d ed. Portsmouth, New Hampshire: Heinemann, 1994, 550 pp.

The author is the founding director of The Teachers College Reading and Writing Project at Columbia University and is the nation's leading advocate for children's literacy. Her writing is wise, passionate, and insightful. Parents will appreciate this book as much as professional educators, and they should particularly appreciate chapter 28, "The Home-School Connection: Composing Literate Lives in Homes and Neighborhoods."

THE READING-WRITING CONNECTION

Cook, Shirley. *On the Loose with Dr. Seuss: Using the Words of Theodor Geisel to Develop Reading, Writing & Thinking Skills.* Nashville, Tennessee: Incentive Publications, 1999, 95 pp.

This wonderful book will renew your children's interest in some of the first books they might have read. Using such popular titles as *Green Eggs and Ham, Yertle the Turtle,* and *The Cat in the Hat,* children will create new endings, add imaginary characters, and expand their vocabulary. The techniques used with the Dr. Seuss books can, of course, be applied to any of the other books that your children are reading.

McGuinness, Carmen and Geoffrey McGuinness. *How to Increase Your Child's Verbal Intelligence: The Language Wise™ Method.* New Haven: Yale University Press, 1999, 269 pp.

Section Two, "The 'Language Wise' Verbal Intelligence Activities," is particularly helpful. It provides a series of practical and challenging activities that build vocabulary, enrich understanding, and improve analytical thinking for students from kindergarten through middle school.

STUDENTS WITH LEARNING DISABILITIES

Mooney, Jonathan and David Cole. *Learning Outside the Lines: Two Ivy League Students with Learning Disabilities and ADHD Give You the Tools for Academic Success and Educational Revolution.* New York: Simon & Schuster, 2000, 286 pp.

Although this book is addressed to older students, the authors offer wise and blunt insights for parents of children who are not succeeding in school. Chapter 7 focuses on the particular challenges that academic writing poses for learning-disabled students who can become paralyzed by the prospect of writing. Confronting the hurtful allegations that poor writers are either stupid or lazy, Mooney and Cole offer practical help to students with learning disabilities. In fact, many of their suggestions on organization and perseverance would be helpful to any student. The fact that these students wrote a book is evidence that learning-disabled students can write successfully. They do not argue for allowing students who have attention deficit disorder or verbal learning disabilities to be exempted from writing tasks, but rather suggest that these students will benefit from a clear series of small steps toward writing success.

IDEA GENERATION

Sweeney, Jacqueline. *Incredible Quotations: 230 Thought-Provoking Quotes with Prompts to Spark Students' Writing, Thinking, and Discussion.* New York: Scholastic Trade, 1997, 64 pp.

Select any page at random from this short collection of quotations and essay starters, and you will be unable to claim, "I can't think of anything to write."

Mariconda, Barbara, and Dea Paoletta Auray. *Super Story-Writing Strategies & Activities: 50 Easy Reproducibles with Mini-Lessons That Help Kids Write Wonderful Dialog, Dazzling Descriptions & Much More! (Grades 3-6).* New York: Scholastic Professional Publications, 2000, 64 pp.

Although this book is intended for teachers, it would provide a treasure trove of summer activities for children or an enjoyable way for parents and children to pass a lazy weekend afternoon. The book contains a superior emphasis on revision strategies and includes many examples to help give reluctant writers a jump-start on their writing.

STUDENT PUBLICATIONS

Melton, David. *Written & Illustrated by . . . : A Revolutionary Two-Brain Approach for Teaching Students How to Write and Illustrate Amazing Books.* Kansas City, Missouri: Landmark Editions, Inc., 1985, 95 pp.

All children should have the pleasure of seeing their work published. This practical book provides step-by-step instruction from brainstorming of topics, to drafting and editing, to final publication. Parents who are wondering how they can help promote literacy in their child's school should consider creating an authors' club or volunteering to help bind and publish books written by young authors.